Baton Change

The Next Generation

Peter Lyne

Dearest John & Margaret,

Wishing you God's richest blessings,

Lots of love,

Peter & linda

Sovereign World

Sovereign World Ltd
PO box 777
Tonbridge
Kent TN11 0ZS

ISBN 1 85240 286 5

This Sovereign World book is distributed in North America by Renew books, a ministry of Gospel Light, Ventura, California, USA. For a free catalog of resources from Renew Books/Gospel Light, please contact your Christian supplies or call 1-800-4-GOSPEL.

Typeset by CRB Associates, Reepham, Norfolk.
Printed in the UK by Clays Ltd, St Ives plc.

Contents

Dedication

To my wife Linda who has worked tirelessly with me on this book, typing, proofing, re-drafting and providing so many valuable insights. Linda has totally shared in my pilgrim journey for 30 years, making huge sacrifices en route. For me, she epitomises the woman described in Proverbs 12:4: *'A wife of noble character is her husband's crown.'*

Since my youth, O God, you have taught me,
and to this day I declare your marvellous deeds.
Even when I am old and grey,
do not forsake me, O God,
*till I declare your power to **the next generation**,*
Your might to all who are to come.

(Psalm 71:17–18)

Acknowledgements

The last seven years at New Generation Church, Sidcup, have been a steep learning curve for us! I want to pay a special tribute to the members of the original 'Acorn Centre' who had faith in us and helped us get re-established in Britain. Mike West and the faithful Leadership Team provided us with generous support and encouragement and facilitated the release described in this story. Also, Gerald Coates and the Pioneer Network of Churches gave us such a warm welcome and a wider sphere of interaction that has proved invaluable. To our dear friends Paul and Paula Weston and their team of new leaders we owe a profound debt of gratitude. As I say in the introduction, this really is their story!

To our friends Adam and Shona Pink-Martin, with whom we share a home in Auckland, special thanks are due. Adam is a 'computer buff' who has saved our bacon again and again and Shona constantly keeps us on our toes with her searching questions.

Special thanks to Chris and Jan Mungeam and all the team at Sovereign World, especially Tim Pettingale for his constant encouragement, valuable advice and friendship.

Foreword

Baton Change is an inspiration. Practical enough to be a handbook for all new generation church planters and wise enough to become a timeless treatise on the true nature of 'church', this is a must read for any spiritual leader with an ambition to plant something powerful and lasting.

Above all this book is honest. There are no platitudes here. We follow a young couple through hilarity and heartbreak as they search for ways to reach cities and build ministries. No disaster is covered up. Instead, painful lessons are recounted to us as they occurred. For this reason, anybody can find hope and wisdom in these pages, from the veteran apostle to the young person with a godly dream in their heart.

I read these pages with growing excitement. I began to realise that I had in my hand a breakthrough book like David Wilkerson's *The Cross and the Switchblade*. Like Wilkerson's classic, this is a self-revealing, accessible story that leads us into the heart of a new generation. As the pages turned, I found myself listing the younger readers that I would give this book to. By the last page, I had added a list of senior pastors.

Well-written, humorous and full of stories, *Baton Change* contains uncomplicated yet explosive truths that could mean new beginnings for many churches. I dare you to sit down, tell God you're willing to follow Him anywhere and then begin to read. Peter and Lynda Lyne exhibit no desire to be fashionably radical. However, their story is full of risks taken and bizarre creativity. Best of all, this is a true account of breakthrough and harvest, an answer to the prayers of everyone who has agonised over this lost generation.

Thank you Jesus. Thank you Peter and Linda.

John Dawson
Founder, International Reconciliation Coalition
Los Angeles

Preface

Baton Change: the most crucial part of a relay race where one highly trained athlete passes the baton to another within a certain space on a running track. If the baton is dropped, if it's not handed over within the proper markings, or if the athlete runs out of their lane, the whole team is immediately disqualified – even though the other athletes have made it round the track successfully. It could all be over because of one mistake. Since the days of the early Church a baton has been passing from one generation to the next. Peter's book will help us to continue the race successfully.

I met Peter Lyne a few years ago and was totally blown away by his style of leadership. His heart was that of a father, a servant, a gatherer, a mentor, and a releaser. It didn't take me long to see something in Peter that I respected. I wanted to serve Peter and quickly started to draw out from him the wealth of information, knowledge and experience that he had as a father of the Charismatic Church. Peter has definitely practised what he preached and he began to father and train me to be able to carry the baton.

As I look around at other churches, networks and global movements, I see within some of them the tragedy of a generation of young emerging leaders that feel that they can do it on their own. They often sprint off too quickly, only to find they have not got the baton in their hands. I also see a generation of older leaders who are full of wisdom, experienced in the art of leadership, who have run the race and have run it well, but are reluctant to let go of the baton. It does seem in the days ahead we need both generations to work together in order to fulfil our corporate destiny. As young men and women we must honour the past in order to create our future. As mothers and fathers we need to see the potential of the sons and daughters, many of whom are able, with training and mentoring, to carry the baton for their generation. It would be disastrous if the mothers and fathers, the pioneers of our faith, go to the grave with all that they have paid such a huge price for.

In this book you will find the real life story of two baton changers who have to learn how to run the race together; who had to train together, who had to get the timing right in order to pass the baton on.

I love the verses in Psalm 144:12–14 in *The Message* that say:

> *'Make our sons in their prime like sturdy oaks, our daughters as shapely and bright as fields of wild flowers. Fill our barns with great harvests, fill our fields with huge flocks, protect us from invasion and exile, eliminate the crime in our streets.'*

This has certainly been a hallmark of Peter's pioneering leadership. It's now that we need to see our sons and daughters released in their prime to fulfil the works of God.

I was privileged to be asked to write the preface for Peter's book. It has been an honour to know Peter and Linda Lyne. They have had an eternal impact on myself and Paula. Sit back and enjoy this book, but not for too long, because the starter has called the runners to the blocks.

Paul Weston
New Generation Church
Sidcup, London

The Warm Up

Last night around midnight I received a thrilling report! The phone rang, and it was Paul Weston, the dynamic young leader of New Generation Church in Sidcup on the edge of London, calling to tell me of some of the remarkable things happening with the church. I was sitting in my home in New Zealand, drinking in every word of this apostolic report.

After a lot of prayer and preparation, the church had pitched a marquee in the park right at the centre of the community. Adjacent to the main road leading into the town, and next to a popular family restaurant, it was an ideal, high profile location. Our team of young evangelists and musicians, backed by the Gideon's Army that the church has become, got to work. Miguel Escobar, a remarkable apostolic figure from Chile, preached each night and the Holy Spirit fell. Paul said that he had never seen anything quite like it! An immigrant builder, Dino, was remarkably healed and gave his life to Christ. His wife Yvonne had worked as a domestic cleaner for a number of families in the church and many had shared the gospel with them. He had been unable to work properly for a long time due to a slipped disc and a trapped sciatic nerve. As he was prayed for he was instantly healed and went to work the next morning. The couple he was working for, who were not Christians, came to the meeting the next evening having been amazed by the transformation in Dino. When prayed for, they were overwhelmed by the power of the Holy Spirit and had to be carried out of the tent. Other members of Dino and Yvonne's family gave themselves to Christ over the weekend.

The Gypsies came too! In our society these people, often called travellers, are ostracised by much of the community, but they heard the gospel gladly! Many of the young people from this sub-culture came. In our youth work they had often proved to be the most disruptive people because of violent and aggressive behaviour, but here they were, responding to the gospel. Paul asked the sister of a group of these more difficult boys to pray for them when they responded to the gospel. She herself was a new Christian and not very sure what to pray, so Paul said 'Why don't you just blow on them and let it be like the breath of God touching them.' As she did this, the power of the Holy Spirit fell on them and they collapsed like skittles in a bowling alley! Having seen them overcome by other 'spirits' in the past, this was a refreshing change. Many of the Gypsies said 'What must we do to join this church?'

On the Saturday morning, a team from the church went to work in the nearby car-park, washing cars, giving out flowers and chocolates, and offering a 'prayer station' for those who had specific prayer requests. Paul said the response was phenomenal. It has to be said that in recent years we have done a lot of free car washing, but this time the tempo seemed to have stepped up. Seventy cars were washed and people were so grateful for the gifts. Many asked for prayer. On the following three nights the tent was packed with about 400 people and others outside. The monthly children's event, 'HQ', saw fifty new children plus parents turn up on Sunday afternoon. This is not Africa! This is hard-nosed, cynical, heathen Britain, where only a small percentage of the population ever go to church. But this is all changing!

The leaders of different local churches also came. The Elders of the local New Frontiers Church called Paul to say that they wanted to pick up the shortfall of the costs incurred for the running of this event. Those who understand the dynamics of this will realise that this unifying of different church leaders in the community may represent the greatest miracle of all. Apart from this gracious offer, Paul said the people gave generously night after night. One evening, he said, there was a bundle of twenty fifty-pound notes tightly rolled up and thrust into the offering bucket!

When my wife Linda and I returned from New Zealand in October 1992 to lead this church, we found a group of about thirty-five faithful, but very disillusioned adults. For some seventeen years they had sought to establish a new church, and over the last two years had been on the point of throwing in the towel. They had seriously looked at closing down a number of times, or simply amalgamating with a larger, more successful work. When they joined the Pioneer Network of Churches, led by Gerald Coates, it was really a last ditch attempt at survival. Through Gerald they learned of our impending return from New Zealand and a relationship was forged that forms much of the background to this book. When Sanballat taunted Nehemiah as he tried to rebuild the walls of Jerusalem he said:

> *'What are those feeble Jews doing? ... can they bring the stones back to life from those heaps of rubble...?'*
> (Nehemiah 4:2)

When we arrived at Acorn Church, as it was formerly called, there were plenty of demons saying just that to God's people. It looked pretty hopeless! During the last seven years we have witnessed a miracle of transformation. Some of this has been by design, but a lot of it by default. We had a crucial role as what Lyle Schaller has defined as 'Change Agents', but we can't take glory for what has happened. Not only has the Holy Spirit done some extraordinary things, but He has raised up a remarkable team of new leaders under Paul and Paula Weston who have worked tirelessly to see this come to pass. This is their story!

A few months ago, I did a survey of our leadership team, and found that the average age was thirty-one years. As this included Ray Carvosso, a father figure in his mid-fifties, you will understand that this is a young team for a church! A bit like Jesus and His disciples! When you see that there is a whole echelon of teenage leaders coming up under them, you will know that something fresh is happening. Our meetings are often led by seventeen and eighteen year olds. Frankly, they have a lot more faith than some of us crusties!

In January 1999 we laid hands on the new leadership team who had already been leading the church for some months. Since then, we have returned to New Zealand pursuing a further call of God on our lives, but I feel it is urgent for me to record here some of the stories and the life-changing principles that have impacted us and the shape of the church in Sidcup. The Church world-wide stands at an all-important cross-roads. Are we going to release the Next Generation? Are we going to accomplish the commission Jesus gave us to sow the nations with the Gospel of the Kingdom? Or are we going to allow ourselves to be stuck in some religious rut, while the world pursues its Gadarene slide into chaos! Someone has said that the only difference between a rut and a grave is the depth!

This book is about change – the baton change. If you have any experience of athletics you will know that in a relay race you may have the four fastest runners on the field, but if the baton change is fumbled, you will lose the race! Christian leaders everywhere want to win this race, but a lot of coaching is required for this to be successfully accomplished. This book is about that process!

As the New Millennium got under way, New Zealand witnessed the most remarkable demonstration of this dynamic that I have ever seen. We were hosting the America's Cup, the International Yacht Race that attracted syndicates from all over the world. In the preliminary competition, all the contenders, including three from the United States were eliminated, leaving the Prada boat from Italy to contest the final with New Zealand. Because New

Zealand were the Cup holders they had not had to race in the preliminary rounds. They now faced a gruelling nine race competition, and tension was running high, as they took to the water in their first race against the Italians. A tremendous sigh of relief, turning to jubilation, swept throughout the nation as it was realised that our 'Black Boat' was far superior to any of the competition that we had seen. The crew, under the superb leadership of Russell Coutts, was like a well oiled machine. In the first four races they confidently swept ahead of the Italians, leaving the fifth race as a potential decider.

Then a remarkable thing happened. During race four, Russell Coutts, by now elevated to super-star status, equalled the world record for skippering a winning boat. Would he complete his victory in race five, returning in triumph to the cheering thousands lining the Auckland harbour, with the spotlight of the world's media trained on him?

A very different scenario unfolded. In disbelief, we watched as Russell handed the wheel to Dean Barker, a younger team member that he had mentored. Then he withdrew to one of the support boats, leaving his protégé to command the winning boat. The response to this sacrificial, self-effacing act, was overwhelming. The vast crowds, reporters and television crews that jammed the Viaduct Basin on their triumphant return could scarcely believe what had happened. The baton was passed with immaculate timing and a style of leadership for the new millennium was graphically portrayed to the watching world. For me, the most touching postscript to this event happened the next day. When Russell Coutts was asked by a television interviewer if he was going for a well-earned rest after the intensive months of preparation for the cup, he said: 'Yes, I'm taking my son on the school camp next week!'

Although the events described in this book have primarily come from our experiences at Sidcup over the last eight years, a seed was firmly planted in my heart during a short visit to England in the late eighties. Gerald Coates had invited me to an Apostolic Team Leader's day at his home in Esher. Of the twenty leaders present, most of them were responsible for heading up the New Church networks that have so dramatically influenced the life of the Church in Britain. After prayer, we began to discuss a pressing issue: **the unreached people groups in the United Kingdom**. As we talked together, this was narrowed down to a more specific unreached people group of great concern to us all: **teenagers**!

It was amazing to hear men like Gerald Coates of Pioneer, Roger Forster of Iccthus, Terry Virgo of New Frontiers, Tony Moreton of Cornerstone, Barney Coombs of Salt and Light Ministries, all confess the same thing. None of their churches were effectively reaching teenagers! If teenagers were present in the church meetings, it was often under sufferance. Perhaps their parents were Elders or still carried sufficient influence to get them there! On the whole, teenagers didn't like our meetings, and were conspicuous by their absence.

That day together birthed something in my heart that has never left me. In subsequent years, when I was invited to speak at various leaders conferences, I would usually ask the same question: 'How many of you are under thirty years of age?'

The answer to this question was invariably disappointing. Knowing that all these Team Leaders, including myself, were plunged into leadership in our early twenties, I wondered what had caused us to change our attitude. Were we now 'playing it safe'? Had risk taking been overtaken by a more structured security?

If you think that the problem of absent teenagers relates to Britain exclusively, think again! I was in the United States in June 2000 and read some alarming statistics in the current issue of *Charisma* Magazine:

> 'Current statistics show that 88% of America's 30 million teenagers don't go to Church. Of the 12% who currently attend church, 80 % will stop attending before they graduate High School.'

> (*Charisma* Magazine, July 2000, p. 39)

These facts alone must serve as a serious 'wake up call' to the Church.

As always with my writing and teaching, this book is arising out of experience. I'm not fond of theories, being essentially a pragmatic person. We make no claim to having all the answers or having done everything right. In fact, there may well be others who have done it better, and we want to learn from them. But this is the story of how one church made a life changing transition from frustration and barrenness, to become a pacesetter for the new millennium. And the good news is: **It's not over yet!**

Chapter 1

Whistle Blower

Years ago a friend of mine, John Noble, said to me: 'You must work with the people God gives to you.' At the time, I was feeling frustrated that the 'new church' we were growing, was not a true reflection of society. Because of our links with the University of Bristol, we were swamped with students. At one time more than sixty percent of the congregation had University degrees and we had at least fifteen medical doctors in training. I thought this was unnatural. How could we more obviously reflect a cross-section of the culture of which we were a part? John said: 'Forget it!' These are the people God has given to you and they reflect something of your own history.' I had been converted as a student and was involved for some years in student missions in many of our British universities and colleges. John went on the say: 'You have a tremendous pool of potential leaders. If it feels unnatural it is because you are training an exceptionally gifted group of people.'

With this wise counsel I came to peace and determined to get on with the job. It was during these early days that we learnt an important foundational principle in the training of potential leaders. Like so much of our future guidance, our inspiration came from the life of Abraham.

During a time of intense conflict, Abraham's nephew Lot and his household were taken captive by a group of invading kings. When Abraham received news of this tragedy, he determined to rescue Lot and his family. To do this:

> '...he called out the 318 trained men born in his house-
> hold...'   (Genesis 14:14)

This was no band of mercenaries, these men were part of his extended family. I don't want to stretch the analogy too far, but during the early days of the church in Bristol, the dynamic of relationships was all-important! Reflecting on this fact some twenty-five years on, I still see this as being an essential, foundational principle in everything we build. It is at this point that the church world-wide fails in understanding the true nature of its calling. Words like **house**, **family**, **body**, and **friends**, that dominate the pages of the New Testament, have become **church buildings**, **church boards**, **organisations**, and **projects**. It's an inter-esting fact that you cannot equate the ministry of Jesus with any of the latter concepts which are now commonplace in the Body of Christ, only with the house, family, body life, and the intimate friendship that were the essential elements of His ministry.

Some years ago, the late Malcolm Muggeridge recorded a series of programmes for BBC Television on the life of Christ. This was prior to his conversion, and during the series he walked around the Holy Land discussing incidents from the Gospels with his old friend, theology professor, Alec Vidler. One statement from Muggeridge made a deep impression on me. He said:

> 'As I walked in the steps of this carpenter from
> Nazareth, I couldn't help but ask the question "What
> does Lambeth Palace and the Vatican have to do with
> all this?"'

It's a valid question! This is not intended to be a diatribe against Anglicanism or Catholicism – or for that matter any other 'ism' – Pentecostal, New Church, or otherwise. What we must recognise if we are to build an effective team, is that the great point of division is between that which is **institutional** and that which is **relational**. Early on God said to us: 'Open your home, share your lives, be a friend!' This is the heart of the church: a dynamic, self-sacrificing community, whose values are at odds with the increasingly self-centred, isolation, of the 'me' generation. According to the Apostle John, the two first disciples to follow Jesus asked a question: *'Rabbi' (which means Teacher) 'where are you staying?'* Jesus reply was: *'Come ... and you will see'* (John 1:38–39).

For many of us, this is the simple key to finding a pool of potential new leaders. We must let them into our lives! This is risky stuff. When we first opened our home back in those early days in Bristol, we didn't realise how vulnerable this would make us. Many came 'to see'; not all liked what they saw, like the friends that came to tell us we had too many house plants and our central heating was five degrees higher than theirs! But enough did stay to form a committed core at the heart of the church with the potential for reproduction. Our first experiences were that all our leaders did similar things: opened their houses, extended their families, shared their lives. We sought to build relationally, even before we fully understood what we were doing.

Since then I have visited churches all over the world and have been frequently surprised by the number of leadership teams and eldership groups who have never been inside one another's homes! And yet most of the qualities listed by Paul as necessary for potential elders and deacons have to do with how these people are at home with their wife and children, their neighbours, work-mates or business partners. Difficult to know, if you only meet at church meetings and elders boards! In fact there is very little in these passages (1 Timothy 3:1–13; Titus 1:5–9), about praying clever prayers and giving a good word! Nor is there anything about having made a lot of money, which seems to be a primary qualification for elevation to eldership in many churches. Unfortunately, a lot of the men and women who have made substantial money in their business or their career, have done so at the expense of their families, and lack the very qualities for church leadership that Paul sees as being essential!

So when Jesus said, 'Follow me' to a bunch of fishermen, tax collectors and the like, and they started wandering around the countryside together, staying in a variety of homes and sometimes camping outside because they couldn't find a bed, He was demonstrating a model of leadership training that is still important for us today. He trained them on the job and taught them as they walked from place to place. He didn't set up 'The Capernaum Bible School', but early on sent them out to heal the sick, cast out demons and proclaim the Kingdom of God. Then they had to come back and tell Him how they had done. Very few theological colleges have healing the sick and casting out demons on their curriculum! Most of the adjustments Jesus sought to make to their character came out of life situations, not sterile classrooms.

There is a very simple rule of thumb here. Leaders have followers! If no one is following you, then I doubt if you are a leader. Even in the teenage gang culture in Sidcup we saw this. If you can get the leader you'll very soon have their followers.

I love to hear Paul Weston give his testimony. When he was converted right out of the world with no Christian background he was part of a group of friends involved in Scouting and other activities. He made the mistake of falling in love with a very determined Christian girl. She didn't say 'no', but she got him powerfully converted before saying 'yes'! When Paul became a Christian it opened a floodgate to all their friends. Meeting to pray and study the Bible became the most natural thing. There was no set time or day of the week – it happened constantly, often until late at night! Within a few weeks at least twenty of those friends became Christians.

The only hiccup to this was when they got 'churched' and well-meaning Christians started to dampen their enthusiasm. Before long, this vibrant, happening, relational group, got split up into church cell groups. I think 'cell' may be an appropriate name for a lot of these groups. They would be more at home in a prison than in the pages of the New Testament. Fortunately, all this has been recovered, but not without a struggle! See Paul and Paula anywhere today and they are surrounded by young people. Go up to the flat that they have been sharing with John, who kindly opened his house to them, and there are always young people there! It may be Justin, camping down in our youth drop in, coming over for his morning shower, or Matt and John, playing on the Nintendo, or one of the teenage girls with boyfriend trouble!

If Paul goes out to speak at a College, as he frequently does, his car is packed with young disciples. They may not know that this is what they are, but it's how Paul is shaping their lives in any and every situation. Paul is 31, about the age of Jesus when He was fulfilling his ministry. I have watched him produce more in five years than most professional ministers produce in a lifetime.

One thing that Paul hated when he got involved with us were 'Leaders Meetings'. Any excuse and he wouldn't come, and if he did, he would often lie on the floor looking decidedly out of it! He saw them as being very wordy, and often indecisive and inconclusive. He would frequently ask us at the end of a long drawn out session, 'What have we decided here?' From his perspective much of it was a waste of time. Some of this related to his own insecurity, but much of the time he was right! I became convinced that God probably hated much of what we were trying to do as well!

Now that Paul is running things, a leaders meeting is as likely to be down at a local pub, or at a nearby coastal resort, as in a church office somewhere. A lot happens in transit. Because his car is always full of people, a traffic jam on the motorway is not a frustration, but a 'sort-out' –a time of prayer, some music, some fun.

Time to blow the whistle

Some years ago, my wife Linda said a profound thing which has never left me. We were having a very difficult and confrontational leaders meeting in our home, and it all got too heavy. She simply got up and left the room. That afternoon she walked for several hours in our favourite park, contemplating all that had transpired. Because it was a beautiful Sunday afternoon the park was alive with activity. Families enjoying a picnic, dog walkers, courting couples, people jogging and whizzing by on roller-blades. When Linda returned she said to me 'They all seemed so happy. Why does the church often make us unhappy?' Of course we know that not all of those people in the park were happy, but when we think of Jesus declaration of purpose: *'I have come that they may have life, and have it to the full'* (John 10:10), we must reflect on the fact that so many of our Christian meetings can be life draining, not life giving! In so many instances it is time for the coach to **blow the whistle** and call 'time out' – or even in some situations 'game over'.

Recently, I was having coffee with the senior partner of a very successful Real Estate company. He told me of his more recent experience in Christian leadership when he was invited to be on the Eldership of a thriving city church. Up until then he had been doing well at his job and enjoying his family. He and his wife had an attractive lifestyle and an open home that drew lots of people, many of whom were not Christians. Suddenly the brakes came on! More and more time had to be spent in Elders meetings, so much so that his partner had to carry the business. Where they had previously had time for hospitality and won many of their neighbours and friends to the Lord, now he was just too tied up in the offices of the church.

Something is very wrong! I know that this story can be repeated again and again. I have lost count of the number of

Christians who have confided in me that within months of their conversion, they lost all their non-Christian friends. Some of this may be as a result of 'the 'offence' of the gospel, but Jesus seemed to give offence mostly to the religious hypocrites, not to the sinners. In the main it's a result of misguided teaching, and the fact that we get sucked into a never-ending round of meetings and projects. John 10:10 has been re-translated: 'I have come that you might have meetings and have them more abundantly'!

Some will say, 'The early Church met every day and we must do the same!' But where did they meet and what were they doing? They weren't sitting in rows, watching a few spiritual professionals perform. They were in and out of the temple courts where the great mass of humanity in Jerusalem was likely to gather, or they were breaking bread in their homes, and eating together with glad and sincere hearts, praising God and enjoying the favours of all the people:

> *'And the Lord added to their number daily those who were being saved.'*   (Acts 2:46–47)

None of this is likely to happen with our closeted Christianity. Our breaking of bread tends to be an artificial religious ceremony tacked on to the end of an equally religious meeting. It's not marketplace stuff. It's not 'Hey you guys living next door, come and hear how my mother-in-law has just been healed! We'll pray for you as well.' Someone has to blow the whistle! We must get the team off the field of play for a while. More likely, we must get the majority of saints out of their seats in the stands where they have been watching others do it, and are now used to waiting for it to be done for them! Many of them would like to be involved. They would like to know what the game plan is, and how they can be a part of it.

In this chapter I've already jumped across a quarter of a century of experience. I started by sharing a foundational principle that we learnt in Olveston, Bristol, that has subsequently shaped all of our thinking. Latterly, I've been seeing that same principle affecting us in the church at Sidcup and in all that is happening through Paul and Paula Weston and their team. The whole of this book will be like this. Drawing from the treasure chest of our experience through nearly thirty-five years of ministry to the present day.

'Promised Land' thinking

Before you switch off and say, 'I'm too old for this, too settled in my ways, or maybe just too comfortable' let me remind you of one of my heroes, Caleb, who has always inspired me. Joshua chapter fourteen is one of my favourite passages of the Bible. Having survived forty years spent wandering in the wilderness as a result of his fellow spies' unbelief, he now gets a crack at the Promised Land. When he and Joshua had been sent into Canaan by Moses they came back with a faith-filled report, unlike the other ten spies that Moses sent with them. They too had been to Hebron and seen the gigantic descendants of Anak. They weren't oblivious to the problems, but were confident that God was with them and would help them possess the territory (Numbers chapters 13 and 14).

On this occasion, the voice of the majority prevailed, and they spent forty years wandering outside of the promise of God until the generation that perpetrated this unbelief had been wiped out.

What kept Caleb going all those years? He had a vision backed by the promise of God. He was prepared to wait for another chance. He said to Joshua:

> '. . . Moses swore to me, "The land on which your feet have walked will be your inheritance and that of your children for ever, because you have followed the LORD my God wholeheartedly."' (Joshua 14:9)

Every day Caleb lived with the feel of that soil beneath his feet and Moses' words ringing in his ears. As he watched his children, then his grandchildren grow up, he said to himself, 'I'm going to get it for you.' He would tell them stories about it and the giants he had seen, and how they were no match for a man of faith, and one day he was going to get those suckers!

Finally, getting into the Promised Land he comes to the Chief of Staff, Joshua, and asks for his inheritance. Did he want a nice retirement village on the shores of Galilee with good fishing rights? No! Listen to what he says:

> 'Now then, just as the LORD promised, he has kept me alive for forty-five years ... So here I am today, eighty-five years old! I am still as strong today as the day Moses sent me out; I'm just as vigorous to go out to battle now as I was then. Now give me this hill country that the LORD promised me that day.' (Joshua 14:10–12a)

This hill country was in fact Hebron. It was the home of that fearful race of gigantic men who first put off Moses' spies from possessing the land. They were still there, gloating over their territory. Caleb had them in his sights for a long, long time! He says to Joshua:

> 'You yourself heard then that the Anakites were there and their cities were large and fortified, but the LORD helping me I will drive them out just as he said.' (Joshua 14:12b)

God said of Caleb that 'he has a different spirit and follows me wholeheartedly' (Numbers 14:24). We need people of a 'different spirit', who have a wholehearted faith. Describing the difference between himself, Joshua and the other ten spies, Caleb said:

> '... my brothers who went up with me made the hearts of the people sink.' (Joshua 14:8)

Almost all church leadership teams have a 'sinker' – sometimes more than one! They will successfully torpedo every faith step the others want to take. The bottom line is that it comes down to this: it's nothing to do with **age**, but everything to do with **attitude**! The successful team will need Caleb's and Joshua's who will help this next generation posses their inheritance.

Chapter 2

Team Spirit

We arrived in Sidcup in October 1992. At the beginning of that year we received a clear direction from the Lord to return to England from our home in Auckland, New Zealand. Our three children planned to join us at Christmas as Amanda and Simon were still finishing studies and Richard had a job. I had visited Sidcup, a suburb on the South East edge of Greater London, just once before. Gerald Coates, the director of the Pioneer Network of Churches, had asked if we would consider helping a church that was newly affiliated to them. After Gerald's initial request, I made a preliminary visit to the Acorn Church as it was then called, while visiting England during the Spring of that year. Although the church had been struggling, I had a definite sense that this was an important step for us, and this was ratified by Gerald and a team of National leaders from around the country, all of whom had known us for many years.

We received a wonderfully warm welcome from the people in Sidcup. They had been faithfully praying for the previous two years in an effort to discover God's will for the church, and to break the spiritual impasse that was very evident. The group consisted of about thirty-five adults with children and a few teenagers, and they met in a former Brethren Chapel, now renamed 'The Acorn Centre'. It has to be said that the level of commitment in this group was quite remarkable considering the struggles they had been facing.

Many things happened during our first year there, but two developments in particular took place that were to dramatically affect our future. I have called this chapter 'Team Spirit' because there can be no doubt that our people at Sidcup had felt disillusioned, and depressed for some time – they seriously needed re-vitalising as a team.

Engaging the enemy

When the Apostle Paul encourages us to: 'Put on the full armour of God' it is because he knows that we have an adversary, one who is determined to frustrate God's plan for His Church if he can. He goes on to say:

> *'For our struggle is not against flesh and blood, but against the rulers, against the authorities, against the powers of this dark world and against the spiritual forces of evil in the heavenly realms.'*   (Ephesians 6:12–18)

These powers and spiritual forces dominate many situations and often go uncontested. This is true both in the Church and in the world, but often in the Church we don't realise how devastating this influence has been. When we do begin to face up to this, it's important for us to engage in both spiritual warfare and a practical antidote to the spirits that have dominated and controlled us. Just take a look at the football leagues. You can have a potentially great team with a squad comprising some very skilled professionals, but if their morale drops, if they lose their buoyant spirit, they can start to lose game after game and nothing seems to go right for them. However, a gifted manager can help to restore the team spirit, provide new strategies and a develop a game plan that will halt the downward spiral.

There were certain things in the history of this church that had stunted its growth, but one particular issue came into focus as we began to pray. We invited a man called

Norman Barnes to meet with us one Sunday and gave him a very specific brief. He was a man who had known the church for some years, but also carried acute prophetic insight. Our request was that he should spend the evening in prayer and prophecy with us. During the days prior to his visit we made special preparations. On the Wednesday we had a day of prayer and fasting, then gathered the church for corporate prayer in the evening. It was a powerful night. As we prayed together in the back room, my wife Linda felt that as a church we must combat a 'spirit of passivity'. The church's origins with the Christian Brethren meant that many had been raised among godly, Bible-believing people, who were accustomed to stifling their emotions, and all too often restraining the work of the Holy Spirit. In response to this, Linda felt we needed to begin a triumphant march all over the building, singing and shouting to the Lord for His deliverance from this blanket of passivity. As we responded to this, we began to feel an immediate sense of break-through.

The following Sunday evening with Norman Barnes and his wife Grace, was quite remarkable. Norman led us in corporate, warfare style intercession, interspersed with prophetic words and exhortations. He demanded that we engage in this as a body of believers, not just one or two of the more vocal individuals. Anytime he felt we were flagging he drew us back to the main focus again. He was like a dog with a bone and was not about to let go! Right in the midst of this, during a time of tumultuous praise, he became very excited. He declared in a stentorian voice:

> 'I can see what it is that has bound the freedom of the Holy Spirit in this church! It's a spirit of passivity coming from your Brethren roots!'

Linda and I had felt it important not to brief Norman on the issues we were considering prior to his coming, so we were all very excited by this. I felt that this was a significant turning point in the life of the church, preparing the way for what was to follow. We had all prayed over and over again and repented of anything that we could think of that might have hindered our progress, but the binding of this spirit that had dogged us required supernatural revelation and authority that would release the church.

I said earlier that it is important for us to engage in both spiritual warfare and a practical antidote to the spirits that have dominated and controlled us. In Luke's Gospel, an incident with Jesus and His wider circle of disciples highlights the need for this. When the seventy-two return from their first mission, excited that 'even the demons submit to us in your name', Jesus replies:

> *'I saw Satan fall like lightning from heaven. I have given you authority to trample on snakes and scorpions and to overcome all the power of the enemy; nothing will harm you. However, do not rejoice that the spirits submit to you, but rejoice that your names are written in heaven.'*
>
> (Luke 10:18–21)

The falling of Satan from heaven in this passage is obviously linked to the mission on earth being accomplished by the disciples. As they did what Jesus commanded them to do – proclaim the Gospel of the Kingdom, heal the sick and cast out demons – so the satanic powers were overthrown from their dominating and controlling position. It needs to be said at this point, because of the secularisation of so much of the Church today, that Jesus was not operating from an inferior psychology. Anyone who takes 'the sword of the spirit, which is the word of God' and begins to wage war in Jesus' name against the principalities and powers, will quickly discover the reality of their dominating and controlling influence in the world today. When the Apostle John declares: 'The whole world lies in the hands of the wicked one' he was stating the truth. However, it is not spiritual warfare alone that will combat these legions. We must have action on the ground. To combat our passivity, we needed a more aggressive response. Ours was to engage in a thrust forward in determined evangelism.

The Hit Squad

Soon after returning to Britain I heard about 'The Hit Squad'. Pioneer had been running a successful programme for some years called 'Tie Teams'. The 'Tie' stood for 'Training in Evangelism'. People of all ages, but mainly young people, would set aside a year of their lives to be specially trained in evangelism. Alongside of all the classroom stuff and church experience, they were exposed to more intensive evangelistic missions. These were affectionately known as 'The Hit Squad' – a name that was not otherwise publicly used. After several discussions with our leadership team we felt the time was right to prepare for such an initiative. It was a daring step for a small church with limited resources to undertake, but looking back, I can see how important this strategy was in our development. To break 'passivity' you must counter it with an opposite spirit, one that is determined to reach out and impact the community, not lie back and wait for better times to come.

I contacted Pete Gilbert, who was himself a gifted evangelist now leading the 'Tie Teams', and our plans began to take shape. A planning team was formed from Peter's associates and key people from our church. We would meet each month for detailed brain-storming and planning, then in the evening of this day, we would gather the church for specific prayer and practical training in evangelism. The idea was that you didn't simply import a team of specialists, but mobilised the whole church to be a part of it. Two weeks were selected mid-summer for our 'hit', and already church members were allocating some of their annual leave so that they could be part of the action.

The plans were ambitious to say the least. The event was to be called 'Design for Life' and we were planning to have at least fifty evangelists focusing on Sidcup for two weeks,

getting into every area of society that we could. The days
would start with car window washing for people on their
way to work and a 'zap' van that targeted crowds of school-
children at the bus stops. There followed School assemblies
and special classroom sessions, door to door visiting and
questionnaires in the High street. Later in the day there
were visits to retirement homes and afternoon teas for
the elderly. Some great home events were planned in the
evenings followed by late night work in the pubs. The list
was never ending and involved an enormous amount of
work. A young woman called Penny Leighton came on
board as a full-time administrator. We would have sunk
without her. Pete enlisted the help of three gifted 'professionals': Steve Lee – comedian, magician, circus and street
performer; Andy Reed – assisting Steve, but also an experienced pub worker; Linda Ward, talented chat-show host
and singer. These formed an important core for our team
and catalysed the church into action.

During the first week, we majored on schools, homes and
street work. For the following week we erected a large
marquee on a playing field close to the railway station.
The marquee hosted a children's club, a daily toddlers event
with a chat show for parents, a circus, a fun day, music
events for teenagers, a cabaret and some preaching and
healing meetings!

An unexpected opportunity came our way just before the
start of Design for Life. I had scoured the High Street
looking at empty shops and called on various landlords to
see if we could rent one for the fortnight. The very last one I
tried was owned by a bank who had recently moved to a
new location. I was amazed when they contacted us to say
that we could have the use of this very suitable building for
next to nothing. The shop was in a strategic position, close
to a notorious pub, and after some days of hard work
transforming the interior, 'Generation X' was born. This
was to be the forerunner of all that we would later do in our
youth work. It was here that we cut our teeth.

To give you an idea of what happened during those two

weeks, let me describe one evening that stands out in my memory. The editor of a regional newspaper had agreed to meet me on the pavement outside Generation X. When he arrived, he talked with me for some time outside the venue about what we were trying to accomplish with the youth. He then went into the packed rooms and interviewed a number of teenagers. He was obviously very impressed, so I asked him if he would like to see something else. It was about 9.00pm and he agreed to walk with me to a Barbecue happening in a nearby street. Two families in the church had adjoining gardens and at least seventy or eighty friends and neighbours were enjoying an outdoor feast with a special programme from the team. We arrived at the moment when Steve Lee was sawing my wife Linda in half! Although this caused quite a stir, it could not account for the incredible atmosphere that was evident. As the journalist didn't seem anxious to leave, I asked him if he would like to see something else. This time, we walked up to the Black Horse, a large pub on Sidcup High Street.

Inside, the public bar areas were jammed with people. We pushed through to the bar and ordered a drink, and as we did so, Ian, the landlord, edged through the crowd and warmly shook my hand. He said, 'Peter, this is the best thing that has happened to us. Your team has had a fantastic impact on this town. If this is church, I want it!'

I introduced him to the journalist and encouraged him to say something for the paper. One of our team, Andy Reed, had done all the leg-work, visiting all the pubs in the town, explaining what we were doing and asking for a spot in the bar at night. Most pubs agreed to have us on the under-standing that it would be entertainment, not preaching. However, we were allowed to have team members present to chat one on one with the customers.

Steve Lee climbed on a stool and commanded the crowd's attention. His blend of humour and conjuring tricks had them eating out of his hand in no time at all. Linda Ward sang a punchy song, then Steve brought out his guillotine and tried to behead a customer! Within minutes of him finishing, the bar was full of tightly knit groups of people talking to members of our team about what was going on. With the journalist standing next to me I had a tremendous opportunity to share the Gospel with the landlord, Ian, and another man standing at the bar. It turned out that Ian had made a public response at a Billy Graham Crusade some years before and had wanted to know how he could find his way back to God!

Needless to say we got a fantastic write up in the local newspaper. It wasn't a superficial piece of journalism, but a genuine attempt to communicate the heart of what we were doing. Since then, we have been featured in the papers many times, but not all of it has been favourably disposed towards us. I remember my reaction after a particularly negative article on the front of our local newspaper, from a journalist who had neither visited us, nor spoken to any of the team. I thought, 'Well, at least they can't ignore us! We are front page news now!'

All through Design for Life we were stretched and challenged. We didn't see vast numbers converted, though there were several people who genuinely came to Christ. Thousands were reached with the message of the Gospel in such a variety of ways. One event saw escapologist Pete Sanderson hanging upside down from a hundred foot crane as he wrestled to escape from a straight jacket. Another glorious summer evening saw a crowd of neighbours and friends meeting in one of the nicer houses in the town. Canapés and drinks were served on the lawn. Two well known professional footballers mingled with the crowd. Recording artist, Caroline Bonnett, performed a live set as the sun dipped in the sky. With everyone grouped around tables or standing on the patio, I shared the Good News that had brought us together. Afterwards, I remained until after midnight talking with a group who were full of questions. It was some six months later that one of these ladies met me in the High Street and told me how an Alpha course in a local church had clinched for her the quest begun in her neighbours back garden that night.

A new name for a new generation

Perhaps the most significant outcome of this time was that the DNA of the church was irreversibly changed! We could no longer be passive about our faith or worship. We were there to impact the community or we might as well not exist! In the run up to Design for Life a significant change took place. We were preparing some excellent publicity that was to be distributed to every home in the town. For some time we had been thinking about the church name 'Acorn'. I love acorns with their unique shape and polished skin, but acorns are small and embryonic. It's the life inside that has to be released and will produce oak trees. As we prepared the publicity, we wanted to change the name, but this suggestion had met with a fair amount of opposition. After one leaders meeting where a majority were giving this the thumbs down, the youth group met at our home the next evening and unanimously agreed that we must take this step. During a united prayer meeting with several other churches in town, our daughter Amanda gave an important prophecy about the New Generation. The leader of the meeting latched onto this theme in the prayers that followed. Many of us who heard the prophecy felt that this should become our new name, and so the Acorn Church became the New Generation Church.

Another spin off from this time had to do with 'Generation X' The success of this venture led us to believe that we should set up a more permanent project for the youth in the town. We went back to the bank, and although it took several months for them to decide, eventually we got use of their High Street premises for another year. Paul Weston, who had been attracted to the original project during Design for Life, agreed to lead this with our daughter Amanda. Our son Richard, who had taken a year off work to train with TIE teams, was also very much involved. We set up a video games arcade, pool room, a non-alcoholic bar, and a dance area with a small stage. Opening on Friday nights, the venue became immensely popular. We were usually packed to the doors and our team had their work cut out managing the volatile crowd.

One day, a senior police officer contacted us saying, 'Do you realise that you have the most dangerous young man in the town coming into your club?' Apparently, this boy was already on several charges of aggravated assault and rape. The police were frustrated because whenever he was charged, people were afraid to testify against him. It's amazing that we escaped any serious incident, especially as my daughter and a number of young women were regularly at the centre until quite late.

One incident that deeply impacted us all concerned a boy of seventeen called Aaron. He was a likeable rogue from one of the Traveller families at the bottom end of town. Several of us built a good rapport with Aaron and had a number of serious talks with him. One night, Linda, Amanda and I walked along the High Street with him when the drop-in had shut. He bought us some 'take away' food and was particularly friendly to us. Shortly after that, tragedy struck. One Friday night he and a friend stole a motor-bike from outside a house in the town. They had drunk a bottle of Vodka between them which was also stolen, and set off in a very reckless fashion down the main road. They overtook a young man in a car who later gave us an eye-witness account of what had happened. They passed him at enormous speed just before a hump-backed bridge at the bottom of a hill. When they hit the bridge, the bike left the road and crashed into a nearby bus-shelter. His friend was killed instantly and Aaron died twenty minutes later from his horrific injuries. The young man who had witnessed the whole thing was himself a committed Christian. He was with Aaron during those vital few moments before he died. A very stunned community was left behind. The next day we joined Aaron's father sitting on the pavement at the scene of the accident, where a floral shrine had been established. He allowed us to pray with him. Amanda visited Aaron's body lying in the mortuary. With the friendship so suddenly extinguished, it took her a long time to get over this. All of us realised more urgently than ever before the issues of life and death that we were confronting as we determined to reach the New Generation.

Chapter 3

Changing Rooms

When Generation X finally closed down we were faced with a dilemma. The Bank's lease on the building had expired and our new landlord wanted to hike the rent to a figure that was way beyond us. During the breathing space, we thought carefully about a new facility. Our attention was drawn to the premises of a printer in the centre of Sidcup. The business had closed down and a 'To let' sign appeared on the front of the building. To be honest, this building had very little to commend it, apart from its location. Had you passed it, the outward appearance would have seemed quite off-putting, but it was situated on the main car park at the back of the High Street right behind McDonalds. This car park was also a busy thoroughfare for pedestrians walking into the centre of the town. Linda and I got together with some of the team and began to focus some determined prayer on the former printing works.

We spent a lot of time surrounding the building and laying hands on its walls. One of the things we have done increasingly is to engage physically as well as spiritually in our prayers. Prayer for us is never a dull, passive thing. Every month before Design for Life we gathered a group from the church and prayer-walked right around the circumference of the town. It was a refreshing walk taking nearly two hours, and down each road we would pray individually with a partner or in small groups. This car park was to be the scene of many outdoor prayer meetings and other evangelistic activities in the years that followed.

At first, our prayers seemed to have no effect. Our approaches to the leasing company were brushed aside. They were looking for a bigger fish, and anyway this whole site adjacent to the High Street had been zoned for a supermarket development designed to rejuvenate the shopping in the High Street.

After many months, during which we watched the building become more and more dilapidated, we finally got a tentative response. The lease offered was ridiculously high and the timing very uncertain. After some negotiations, we managed to reduce the lease to a third of what they were demanding and arrived at a still very tenuous arrangement. We could have the building for three months up until Christmas and possibly on a month-to-month basis after that. The lease was going to stretch our limited resources as a church still further and we had no idea what it would cost to renovate the premises, let alone to run them. At any time the council could bring things to a halt with some fresh planning constraints.

Faced by all these obstacles the temptation was strong to walk away from the idea. When we finally got through the door the temptation was even stronger! It was worse than a pig sty – especially since most pigs are very tidy compared to the sight that greeted us! Everything was broken, hanging down from the ceiling or lying on the floor. There were heaps of rubbish everywhere. Worst of all a thick, black grease left by the printers covered a large part of the floor area and unknown to us, would require professional contractors to remove it. Even then a residue would try to seep up through the concrete floor in the ensuing months! The toilets were unspeakable and the building lacked any architectural merit. Facing all this, it seemed ridiculous to even begin attacking the problem. But we were full of faith, confident that this was where God wanted us to be – well, some of us were!

A transformation takes place

The Bible says, *'Without faith it is impossible to please God'*
(Hebrews 11:6). At this moment **only** a God-given faith
could have caused us to proceed. The chips were heavily
stacked against us.

I am glad that we have photographic evidence of the
'before' and 'after' in this story, because you would never
have believed the transformation that took place unless you
saw it. A dedicated team got to work. God had blessed us
with a number of very creative people who carried a vision.
Although this place was a dump by most human standards,
they saw how it could be adapted to the kind of venue that
youth would feel comfortable with. Instead of trying to
change what it was – a printing works – they stayed with the
industrial theme, and eventually called it 'The Worx'. Good
use was made of the ugly pillars and the hideous windows
were camouflaged so that there was total black out. Bold
colours were used and special lighting effects. The front of a
truck was used to make a drinks bar with flashing head-
lights. Justin, our crazy designer, built furniture from car
tyres. A pub gave us loads of circular tables and bar stools
and we managed to acquire all kinds of paint and gear at
knockdown prices. We set up an arcade of video games
through a contractor who hoped to make a profit. I'm not
sure that he ever did!

One by one, seemingly insurmountable obstacles were
overcome. This was not without a phenomenal amount of
dedicated hard work. A number of the team got sick from
the fumes given off by the paint. Local interest was aroused
as they saw the work going on. Finally, a deadline was set
and an opening night agreed upon.

Our first 'Worx' project was to be a night-club for
teenagers aged 14–18 years on Friday evenings, and we
endeavoured to be alcohol free. Police asked that we let the
youth smoke inside the building as the potential for trouble
making was far greater when they gathered outside in
groups. This whole experience was a steep learning curve

for us all. The first Friday we did a dummy run with virtually no advertising, and nearly seventy young people came. The next week, this doubled to about one hundred and forty. By the third week, nearly three hundred turned up and crammed into a building that could barely cope with more than two hundred. The following week, the police had to get involved, as there were more outside than in. The crowd that couldn't get inside were causing trouble in the High Street.

Later, the Inspector of Police told us that if he had had ten units of officers available that night he still couldn't have arrested everybody. A good relationship developed with the police who were encouraged by what we were doing, and they have maintained a healthy, supportive relationship ever since. Only recently we received a letter from Inspector Tim Hawkins of the Sidcup Police in which he said: 'The world needs people like you.'

Soon after we opened we had to introduce a body search for everyone coming into The Worx to uncover any covert drugs, alcohol or weapons. This procedure was established because of an experience we had on one of the clubs first nights. Paula Weston was booking in a young man at the door and noticed something protruding out of his sleeve. On further examination it was discovered that he had an iron bar concealed in his coat. Around the same time, because of the numbers trying to get in, one of the older members of our team, Chris Lowth, set up a computer membership list. From his work as a computer consultant he managed to source several second-hand computers and very soon there were a thousand names and addresses on file.

We quickly found that it was necessary to have a team of at least thirty helpers on deck each week. Some were on security duty inside and outside the building, some manning decks, lights and video, others doing bar duty and cloakroom management. People were praying before, during and after the events. We encouraged as much detached youth work as possible – over the pool tables, sitting on the tyre seats, chatting at the door. Frequently things got wrecked. There seems to be a major spirit of violence and lawlessness at large among many teenagers. On the very first night the hand basins were ripped off the wall in the boy's toilets. Others would punch their fists through the plasterboard walls. Sometimes they punched each other and on occasions members of our team as well!

One night, Ray, who was our head of security, asked me to get my car near the back door. A group of youths had come in from an estate some way from Sidcup and were being targeted for trouble. Some of the local gangs are highly territorial. These guys had been threatened several times and wanted to get away quietly. I backed my car up adjacent to the rear exit. Unfortunately, some of the predators managed to crash out of the front entrance and tore round the side of the building to where I had a group of these frightened guys in the car. They banged on the windows, trying to break them and kicked the car. One, spread-eagled himself on my bonnet, and I decided nevertheless to take off with him clinging to my windscreen wipers! As we accelerated down the lane we came to a very tight ninety-degree bend. I swung the wheel sharply and we quickly lost our unwanted passenger who cannoned off to the side. I felt like I was in an episode of Starsky and Hutch! Interestingly enough, the boy spread-eagled on my bonnet was one of a group who came to apologise to us the following week for their behaviour. I quietly resolved to park further away from the building in future!

The incidents surrounding these lost young people abound. Some are vivid in my memory. One night, walking across the car-park, I was called by a group of young people surrounding a girl of fourteen who had collapsed on some waste ground. We managed to get a name from one of the bystanders and were able to run a quick computer check. While one of the team called the girls parents, I sought to assist the girl and find out what had happened. Apparently, she had just had a row with her boyfriend who had broken up with her. Her response was to swallow the best part of a bottle of vodka at which point she passed out, frothing at the mouth. Apparently, she hadn't eaten for two days.

Fortunately, the mother of the girl had been contacted on the phone and arrived in a very agitated state at the car-park. We carried the girl to her car and I accompanied them to the hospital where they gave her some emergency treatment with a stomach pump. In the car en route to the hospital the mother questioned me very closely. When I mentioned the boyfriend trouble, she said, 'But she hasn't got a boyfriend'!

Neither could she understand where her daughter had obtained the vodka. I explained that many stores in our area were selling alcohol illegally to minors, in spite of all our efforts and the attempts of an over-stretched Police force, to stop it. As I talked to this lady it was quite evident, like so many parents, that she was oblivious to what was happening to her child. Fortunately, the girl made a good recovery and her mother telephoned me the next day, thanking me profusely for what we had done. It has been known for teenagers to die in these circumstances.

As The Worx became more established, so a number of developments took place. We managed to extend our lease which finally answered the frequent criticism: 'Why are you doing all this for just three months?'

Around us a supermarket war was taking place. The American giant, Safeway, got the approval and backing of the council and were all set to begin to develop the site. However, Sainsbury's, a huge British chain, badly wanted the site too. They had quietly gone around buying up all the property adjacent to the land including our building. As the day of our eviction got nearer, they lodged a legal challenge to the proposal and the conflict has ensued ever since. We have now occupied The Worx for three years and established a strong rapport with the community.

However, even this has not been without opposition. Our local free newspaper, distributed to every home in the area, carried an inflammatory headline: 'Worx branded a nuisance.'

The lead writer, Linda Piper, had written the story based on one complaint in the written minutes of a council meeting. Shortly after this we were invited to address a cross-section of several public agencies gathered at the Council Chambers. Since then, we have been represented at all of these meetings and just recently, because the Council Buildings were sold to a Family Restaurant developer, the Sidcup Sector meetings as they are called, now meet at our church administrative centre. A lot of goodwill has resulted.

One experience was a real eye-opener for me. I was invited to attend a specially convened meeting at the local Council headquarters and was not entirely sure what the reason for this was. On arrival at the Council chambers I found a variety of people present representing different groups. These were Council Members, Fire Officers, and representatives of the Police and Youth Services.

The meeting hadn't been going long when I suddenly discovered that we were the focal point of attention. The initial question went something like this:

> 'The council has all sorts of Youth initiatives which they are funding with paid professional staff, but attendance at the Youth Centres, for example, has seriously declined. Your group on the other hand has voluntary workers and the backing of a local church, but the youth are coming to your projects while they seem to be boycotting ours'!

For the next hour the questions focused on Generation X and The Worx, and what the secret of our success was – limited as we perceived this to be.

A second meeting was convened and I took two of the young people who had been helped by The Worx along with me this time. It was interesting to have a magistrate cross-examine one of these guys who had previously been in trouble with the police.

The issues raised by my meetings with these public bodies

is not dissimilar to those that I described in Chapter 1 as confronting the Church. The more institutional and bureaucratic society becomes, the less likely it is that the new generation will relate to it at all! Relational building is still the name of the game in every area of society.

Paul Weston highlighted this problem for me after he had visited another church with a fairly similar ethos to our own. Generation Church in Ewell, Surrey, also part of the Pioneer Network, had been running a heap of successful youth initiatives for years. They took Paul to see the newly opened Youth Centre paid for by the Council and with a staff of fully supported workers. Paul said the design of the place was tragic – chintz Laura Ashley curtains and dated décor – bearing no relation to today's youth. Even more tragic was the handful of youth that frequented the centre! This story can be repeated over and over again. Council meetings, I have found, are full of talk but very little action. Does this sound familiar? As we have continued all of our youth initiatives I'm not aware that we have received a penny from public funds – and yet even Oliur, the owner of the local Indian Restaurant, supplied a set of shirts for our football team!

Out of the initial drop-in project, which ran for more than a year in this form, hundreds of teenagers were contacted. A core of youth were converted and have become part of the new Worx cells where they are being discipled. Gradually The Worx has been used for a greater variety of initiatives, and especially as a centre for prayer. I think I can safely say that this has been the most prayed-in building in my experience of church life.

A children's club called 'HQ' has now also been running for two years. There are regular community contact days involving free car-washing and other activities. One Christmas, a children's musical was staged for three nights. Linda wrote and directed this and was thrilled to see the enthusiastic reception it got. Each night was packed with a number of special guests being ferried to the show from the many Retirement homes in the area. Last Christmas a big street fair organised by the local traders finished up at The Worx for hot pies, mulled wine and a performance by Steve Legg a professional escapologist and magician.

There have been lots of bands, prayer events, gatherings of the church, cabaret-style dinners, and still young people drop in to play pool, ride their mountain bikes or chat to someone. When we literally 'changed rooms' we changed the whole ethos of the church. Our new environment had a dramatic effect on everything we did and gave us a much more strategic position. We moved from a back street location to a facility at the heart of the community. It put us on the map. We still use our former building as an excellent administration centre, toddlers club and seminar venue, but even this facility has been given a dramatic facelift to reflect the change in the culture of our church. The Worx development pushed us out into the public arena like nothing else could.

Chapter 4

Talent Spotting

When I first met Paul Weston, he and his wife Paula had been passing through a period of disillusionment. Like many people I meet, especially in these 'post charismatic' years, they loved God but were really struggling with the Church. They had been involved with a large Charismatic church in which they had led a thriving youth ministry, but the work they were doing often seemed at odds with the wishes of the Eldership. Gradually it became more difficult for them to function in this environment and they were asked to lay down their leadership. I don't wish to pass judgement on this decision because it was made by good, well-meaning people, who I count as friends. It's just that what Paul and Paula were trying to do was moving in a different direction to the mainstream of the Church. This scenario is being repeated in countless churches across the world today, and I wish to address the tension that is caused by this in a later chapter.

I had heard in some round-about way, that Paul had left his job and was determined to take steps of faith to pursue God's call on his life. I remember inviting them round to our house one day so that Linda and I could encourage them in this radical decision. Having made a similar faith step myself when I was only twenty years old, I knew something of the challenge, excitement and the battles that lay ahead of them. We wanted to pray with them and support them in the decision they had made.

One thing we recall from this early meeting with Paul and Paula was that we instantly liked them. I had met them before, but sitting down and spending time with them, we caught something of their infectious spirit and had such a powerful sense of the hand of God being on them. The more we talked, the more I thought of David in the Old Testament and his time at the Cave of Adullam. In fact, the next day I wrote a card with a word from this story on it and sent it to Paul and Paula.

The events of this period of David's life can teach us some valuable lessons about the inherent dangers of baton changing, and we would do well to study and learn from them.

1. The baton change may be rejected

When David was anointed to be king by Samuel, and then subsequently defeated Goliath before the armies of Israel and the Philistines, you would have thought that all his numbers had come up and he had won the lottery. However, it wasn't long after the cheering had died down before Israel's reigning monarch, King Saul, began to eye him with suspicion and a deadly, demonic hatred and jealously overwhelmed him. During his frequent rages he regularly tried to kill David! Saul too had been anointed by Samuel and with his handsome appearance and extraordinary physique, seemed sure to succeed. Like David he assumed power through a notable military victory (1 Samuel 11), but somehow he lost his way and became a tragic failure, the symbol of a lost anointing. He had no desire to pass the baton to David and retire from the race, but he was forced to do so.

David, having become the rising superstar, suddenly finds himself on the run, an outlaw in fear of his life. In spite of the sworn allegiance of Saul's son Jonathan, it became impossible for David to continue his role as army commander. He headed for the hills and set up a guerrilla camp in the Cave of Adullam (1 Samuel 22:1–3).

2. The baton change can be cataclysmic

I love this Adullam story! When the news got out, first of all David's family, including his father's household and his brothers, went down to join him there. By now they were in danger from Saul as well. After that there was a steady drift of all the most unsuitable people!

> 'All those who were in **distress** or were in **debt** or **discontented** gathered round him, and he became their leader. About four hundred men were with him.'
>
> (1 Samuel 22:2)

In normal circumstances a situation like this, comprising these disgruntled people, should have ended in chaos. In fact, what happened here was that this unspectacular nucleus became the core of David's fighting band – the nucleus of an army that would eventually put him on the throne.

Here is a classic example of cataclysmic change. We would hope that in terms of generational transfer in the Church today that it wouldn't be as traumatic as this! Sadly, it often is and there are many reasons for this, not least of which are a 'Saul' who has lost his anointing threatened by a freshly empowered 'David'!

Or it may be the clash of cultures that necessitates this change, not necessarily an autocratic leader. People are often labelled 'rebellious' or 'insubordinate' when they are actually pursuing a fresh vision.

3. The baton change is inevitable

No matter how we may try to hold on to a position of leadership, when God's time comes for us to move on, nothing can reverse it. It is important to recognise the emergence of a 'David' and not allow ourselves to become 'Sauls', holding on to what we have and denying the obvious fact that God's purposes have moved on.

In the case of David at Adullam, three important principles are evident, and failure to recognise them will result
in certain disaster:

1.   He was anointed for the task. God was with him.
2.   There was a relational core at the heart of his team.
3.   The people gathered to his leadership.

If you take on a group of disgruntled people without this
relational buffer, you will be quickly swamped with their
problems. The four hundred *'gathered round him and he
became their leader.'* Without commitment and leadership
you will build nothing that will last. There is often a lot of
super-spiritual talk these days, suggesting that we don't
need leadership. 'Aren't we all kings and priests to God' is
an attitude that is frequently expressed. The truth is, we've
always needed leadership, and the copious examples from
both Old and New Testament support this. However, we do
need different kinds of leadership and team models today if
we are going to effectively meet the challenge of this hour.

Gathering lost sheep

There's another lesson to learn from the Cave of Adullam.
As we have seen, a new leader with a fresh vision will
usually attract a number of dissatisfied followers, eager for
new challenges and input.

If we apply this scenario to church life, we find ourselves
experiencing what church growth guru's term, often
disparagingly, 'transfer growth'. In other words, a church
may be exhibiting substantial new growth, but not all of
this increase has come from new Christians being added
from the outside. This leads some leaders to speak passion-
ately against 'sheep stealing'.

I think there are several valid reactions to this arising
from Jesus' own leadership model. In John chapter 10 he
says, *'His sheep follow him* [the shepherd] *because they know
his voice'*, and *'they will never follow a stranger; in fact, they will*

run away from him because they do not recognise a stranger's voice' (John 10:4–5).

If your sheep can be stolen, were they 'your sheep' in the first place! If they quickly run to a stranger's voice are they worth having anyway?

Another pertinent passage is in Matthew chapter 9 . Jesus is travelling from one town or village to another, preaching in all the synagogues and healing the sick. And *'when he saw the crowds, he had compassion on them, because they were harassed and helpless, like sheep without a shepherd'* (Matthew 9:36).

When we see vast numbers of shepherdless sheep today, should we not similarly have compassion on them? Jesus didn't simply say: 'By the way, there's a good synagogue down the road, don't bother following Me!'

Similarly, David honoured the anointing that was on Saul by refusing to kill him on at least two occasions, but he never submitted to Saul's leadership. Every fresh move of God demonstrates a similar scenario, and while it's true that sometimes unwise, fleshly and unnecessary things happen, most of it is inevitable. Interestingly enough, Adullam means 'resting place', reminding us of Jesus' words:

> *'Come to me all you who are weary and burdened, and I will give you rest.'* (Matthew 11:28)

Coaching lessons

It wasn't long after Paul and Paula got involved with us, that I began to struggle with aspects of Paul's character. He was very restless, often finding it difficult to stay in any church meeting. I would look for him to participate in a meeting, only to find he wasn't there. He wasn't a great time-keeper either, in fact he would have been more at home in an Aboriginal tribe that we once visited, where time wasn't considered important! Being a very structured individual myself, I began to get more and more frustrated with this. In reality, we were probably both on a 'different page' at this time. I came from a background of intense worship and long talks, while Paul was working with youth who could cope with neither. Leadership meetings, that I saw as very important, diverted him from time he wanted to spend hanging out with the youth he was desperate to reach.

Things came to a head. Paul was leading a youth group in the church, but I was so concerned about his apparent lack of discipline (from my perspective), that I felt I should ask him to lay it down. It didn't help that Linda and I were leaving for more than a month of ministry overseas at this time and I felt it necessary to explain what we were doing to the Youth Group Paul was responsible for.

This was a very painful time for Paul and Paula and members of their family and friends. It looked very much like an 'action replay' from his previous church experience. When Paul was at a low ebb in all this, he poured out his troubles to Maddy his mother-in-law, a very skilful counsellor and friend. She was so concerned that she called one of the leaders who was chairman of the team while I was away. He said, 'I can give you Peter's fax number'!

'I don't want a bloody fax number'! she thundered.

Feelings were running high!

When we returned from our time overseas, a very interesting scenario presented itself. Although deeply hurt by what I had done, Paul had humbled himself and given full-on service to the church in our absence. We had a profound time of 'sorting out' during which we confessed our faults to one another.

In retrospect, I shouldn't have handled it the way I did, even though I was very frustrated. The last thing I wanted to do was hurt Paul, but something very special emerged out of this difficult time. I knew I could trust Paul and that he would make a great leader.

Breaking the mould

Most people treated like this would have taken umbrage and left, bad mouthing me in the process. It was the way in which Paul responded to this discipline – and frankly, humiliation – that gave me faith in him and hope for his future. Jeff Lucas, speaking at a recent Pioneer event, said this: 'We all have fault-lines.'

He was talking about Gideon in the book of Judges at the time, a great leader, but with very evident weaknesses. Having lived for so long in New Zealand I am aware that we sit on major fault lines in this country that have been, and no doubt will be, subject to earthquakes and volcanic eruption. A willingness to face our fault-lines and to be ready for mutual adjustment is so critical to team building.

Some time after this, an incident occurred that has subsequently shaped so much of our thinking and practice. Linda and I visited a Pioneer Team day in Guilford with our friends David and Dale Garratt who were staying with us at the time. During the morning session I received one of those *rhema* words that was totally unrelated to what was going on in the meeting. I was thinking about Paul and the Holy Spirit simply said to me: 'He won't fit the mould!'

From that moment on my whole attitude towards Paul changed. I realised that I had a preconceived 'mould', that our church, as a result, was set in a particular 'mould', and that Paul wasn't going to fit it! It's funny, isn't it? Pioneer had hosted a conference week a couple of years prior to this called 'Breaking the Mould'! I wonder how many 'moulds' were demolished during that conference? Mine certainly wasn't.

Theories are great, but we have to find a point at which the rubber hits the road for us. All over the world, churches are encased in moulds and some are mouldier than others! Some are more like straight-jackets. It takes courage to get to grips with this and forge a new way forward – a kind of courage that is often singularly lacking in established church leadership. One church had already lost Paul Weston – possibly their most valuable asset – and I came close to doing the same!

If we're trapped in a particular mould, we'll never have eyes to see the team that God is providing for us. We can spend our lives appeasing the Saul's of this world, while the David's have to run for their lives. Often, I've looked at the twelve that Jesus chose after a night of prayer alone with His heavenly father and thought: 'Would I have chosen them?'

Peter with his big mouth; Thomas with his doubts; James and John with their vindictive, violent streak, and Judas with his money grabbing. Yet, Jesus saw the potential in these people and entrusted the whole of His future plans to them.

Later on as the book of Acts charts the progress of the emerging Church, we find that the most hate-filled of all the Christian persecutors is in fact God's chosen instrument for the evangelisation of the Gentile world! Had you been among the saints in Jerusalem, dragged from their homes and imprisoned by (another) Saul (Acts 8:3), would you have had any inkling that this was the man that God was going to use to crack the heart of the Roman Empire with the gospel?

The great pioneer of the Congo Evangelistic Mission, W.F.P Burton, once told me: 'Go for the worst!' He backed this up from the story of Jesus and the woman of Samaria in John chapter 4. It's not surprising to me that today we hear such remarkable stories of revival occurring in the prisons of Britain and among the Gypsies. Outcasts seem to be high on God's agenda.

At another Pioneer Team Day, a further incident occurred that has a humorous side to it. Dale Gentry, a remarkable prophet from Fort Worth, Texas, was spending some time praying and prophesying with us. I didn't know Dale well at the time, but he called me out from the group and prophesied to me. He said repeatedly:

'John Wayne of the Church in Britain, John Wayne of the Church in Britain. Always looking for a fight, always looking for a fight ... ' etc.

Then he said:

'I see you surrounded by disreputable characters.'

I don't think Paul and Paula and the team have ever forgiven me for this one, as I like reminding them of Dale's word! But in the eyes of the religious hierarchy in Jesus' day, He was always surrounded by disreputable characters, as was His ancestor David.

Following our time of conflict that I have shared frankly about here, Paul and I moved on to a new level of friendship and trust. I regard him like a son and am very proud of all that he is accomplishing for the Kingdom of God. As our years in Sidcup passed by, Linda and I we were more and more out of town, and Paul carried an increasing level of responsibility in the church. Taking us to the airport in his car, he would always get a last minute series of instructions from Linda, ranging from watering the plants to the colour scheme in the church offices. When he picked us up again, he always had a full report to give, so often loaded with good things that God had been doing in our absence. I know that things were not always easy for Paul, and at times I didn't provide everything he needed, but I knew instinctively, in the words of John the Baptist:

'He must become greater; I must become less.'
(John 3:30)

Most great coaches were very gifted players in their youth, but there inevitably comes a time when they must let go and let others run with the ball. When we laid hands on Paul and Paula and their Team in January 1999, I knew that the time had come to let them get on with it.

Chapter 5

Changing Tactics

New teams will require fresh strategies. This is not simply change for the sake of change, but our response to a pressing need. Everywhere I travel amongst the Church world-wide I hear a similar story. People are tired of the 'mixture as before'! The meetings have become so predictable. Tried formulas are being reproduced 'ad infinitum' with few people having the courage to say, 'Why are we doing this?'

Take that staple ingredient of any good Christian's diet, the meeting, for example. Charismatic Christians everywhere have rejoiced in their new found freedom, no longer shackled to liturgies or hymn sandwiches, depending on where they have come from in the Church spectrum. Now they can enjoy endless repetitive singing, followed by even longer talks! I'm deliberately painting a 'worst case' scenario here, and these comments may provoke a hostile reaction, but worship leaders and preachers alike need to know just how boring they can be. Instead of the multi-faceted splendour of stained glass windows and soaring fanned vaulting, our meetings often resemble a very drab council housing estate where no-one cared enough to create an attractive environment.

One night at Sidcup we learnt a salutary lesson. Through our youth drop-in, a teenage tearaway named Richard had been converted. What's more, he was desperate to be baptised. For this sacrament we moved from the funky, converted factory surroundings of 'The Worx' where the youth met, to the bland building we used for some of our meetings – formally a Brethren Chapel. This building had a baptistry set in the floor so that those who professed faith in Jesus could 'follow him through the waters' – though I can't imagine the River Jordan looked anything like this!

When Richard arrived for his baptism with his shaved head and body-piercing, he brought with him some forty of his friends and relatives, eager to see what would take place. We did the baptism early in the meeting in case the attention flagged. It was excellent, with very real testimony and a variety of contributions from the people packed around the pool. The visitors coped well, but when Richard went out to change from his wet clothes after we had prayed for him, all his tribe went with him! They dived into the refreshments in the kitchen and had a whale of a time, while we carried resolutely on with our meeting! Not many churches get forty, raw, unsaved people into their meeting at one hit. We did and we completely blew it. Instead of cancelling our programme we sweetly carried on singing, praying and preaching, while the 'lost' we were desperate to reach had a good time without us! After this debacle, Paul Weston said to me, 'Never again'!

This skirmish with the unchurched taught us a bigger lesson. If they weren't too enamoured with our meetings, could the faithful admit that they weren't ecstatic either?

Bill Hybels, dynamic pastor of the Willow Creek Church in Chicago, has taught us a lot about the church being 'seeker sensitive'. They host phenomenal performance-style events at the church as a shop-window for friends and contacts. This can be a very effective evangelistic tool, provided that what follows on from this in the seeker's church experience is not a huge anticlimax. I know that Bill and his team always thoroughly critique what they have done. It wouldn't hurt us to run a video camera over our average meeting and then take a long hard look at how it sounds and the impression it gives.

When we put the running of meetings into the hands of Paul and Paula and their team, you never knew what would happen next! Inspired by a number of very creative people, things took on a very different shape. A theatre director, Pete Summers, and his wife Emma, a ceramic sculptor, made an offering of a play at Christmas time one year. Pete had been out in a spiritual wilderness for some time and this was his way of saying: 'I want to be back with God and His people.'

It was called 'A.D.' and it involved pretty well everyone in the church. Looking back, I can see how this whole project dramatically influenced what we were to do in the future.

It was not a traditional play with a Christmas theme, but centred on an archaeological dig, where ancient Christian symbols were discovered in the floor of the ruins. The baptistry became the archaeological dig site and spanning out from this, the whole building was transformed to include a number of tableau. This was not a play you simply sat and watched – you entered into it and became part of the drama.

On arrival, everyone gathered in a back room for a welcome and explanation. We were then shepherded round the side of the building to enter the main set. Internally, it looked nothing like our familiar meeting place. Completely darkened, you walked over piles of broken stones to get in. A gripping multi-media script ensued, moving from symbol to symbol related to the discovery at the dig. When this part of the performance was over, everyone moved back into the rear of the building to eat Jewish Passover food, drink wine and talk about what they had experienced. The three nights we did this were well received by the many visitors that came, but an unexpected spin off was that it prepared the way for much that was to follow.

We found ourselves increasingly wanting to reach a generation used to the short, sharp sound bites of television, and the virtual reality of computer graphics. Many of these younger people don't read books, often have a short attention span, and we found that an increasing number through The Worx could not read or write. Some of the Scripture Union material and the Youth Alpha Course for example, seemed to assume a level of literacy and rational thought that was beyond our constituency.

When we tried to absorb them into existing meeting structures it was often chaotic. Have you ever tried speaking for any sustained length of time to a group containing youth who just can't sit still, and simply must go out for a smoke or to visit the toilets? They do nothing quietly and often elicit a group response – if one goes out they all go out, doors banging on the way, and get up to all sorts of mischief when out of sight.

One early experience was with Pete and Jan, the couple who set out the refreshments. They got out to the kitchen to find that everything had been devoured and a mess made of all their ordered cups and glasses. We understood how easy it is to get upset by these things, but all of us needed reminding that the young people were worth a few packets of biscuits and some spilt drinks! We really did want them there, not somewhere else.

One more vulnerable young man made an emergency call on the church office phone which resulted in the police storming into the middle of our worship meeting. This same lad ran up a bill of five hundred pounds on a mobile phone making random calls to America. The company, who had been assured that the church would cover all charges, sent us the bill and were upset to discover that they had been misled. Later, this same young man stole a crucial part of our PA system which we fortunately recovered.

As The Worx got under way, so a transformation took place in our church meetings. We rarely ever met on a Sunday morning anyway, but Sunday evenings took on an exciting new flavour. We can all recall different milestones in this process. I remember the evening we entered the valley of dry bones! The whole evening was centred around Ezekiel's great prophecy of a restored House of Israel (Ezekiel 37:1–14).

As we entered our building, someone had created a dark

valley with suspended black sheets. The lighting was very subdued and lots of children were painted as luminous skeletons. You never got bored in these meetings and the word of God came alive! On this evening it was as if we corporately entered Ezekiel's prophecy, and of course, concluded by praying for a fresh encounter with the 'breath of God' for everyone there.

Another evening saw a running track set up and the whole theme of 'Running the Race' in the New Testament was developed. People had to participate in various kinds of relays. It was a lot of fun but packed with truth. Another evening, that some didn't find so funny, was when we arrived to find our building closed down. Workmen were in the street wearing hard-hats. They had set up barriers and flashing lights, declaring the building unsafe and re-directing us to another venue. The workers were members of the team and when Paul re-assembled everyone, he challenged us to recognise what our security was really in. How would we fare in a country under persecution, where the church had to meet in secret, often moving at a moments notice?

This kind of meeting was not a temporary diversion. We re-shaped the whole of our thinking as to how the church should meet, and lest you think these are merely gimmicks, lacking any enduring quality, let me highlight some of the principles that were established as a result of this.

1. We are the Body of Christ!

Previous centuries saw generations of families deploy their creative gifts in the worship of God. The great Cathedrals of Europe didn't just happen. Skilled architects and builders, stonemasons and engravers, artists and musicians, gave the whole of their lives to expressing the glory of God through their creative gifts. We now understand that Church is not a building, that we are:

> *'Living stones ... being built into a spiritual house to be a*
> *holy priesthood, offering spiritual sacrifices acceptable to*
> *God through Jesus Christ.'*   (1 Peter 2:5)

Like those ancient craftsmen and women, we must deploy all our creative skills to the glory of God.

2. The church must be interactive

Returning to New Zealand after nearly seven years back in London, I have been struck once again by how stereotyped church meetings have become. People sit or stand in rows, looking at pulpits and platforms, where one or more appointed professionals do the stuff. This is a far cry from the spontaneity and life that is evident throughout the New Testament. The formalising of Christian worship has done much to kill the effervescent life of the Body of Christ. The false divisions between sacred and secular, priesthood and laity, have effectively crippled the Church. The word 'laity' means 'a people chosen by God'. To see **everyone** released in ministry is a goal that we are now constantly striving for.

3. The building must serve the worship, not inhibit it

In the early days of the House Church Movement in Britain, it was refreshing to meet in one another's homes. The warmth and hospitality of the domestic setting was conducive to fellowship and the size of the average lounge meant you couldn't avoid eye contact and involvement with each other. As these groups grew in size, most houses in Britain couldn't contain them. In many instances, school halls and classrooms were hired. Try getting inspired in them! All you need is a cold morning in winter and a disgruntled caretaker to dampen your enthusiasm for charismatic worship forever!

Pooling their creative skills, our team learnt to swiftly change our environment in order to assist the whole process of worship and fellowship. Chairs and pews, especially those that are bolted down, are a killer! When we started removing the chairs altogether, we thought we were being innovative. However, my wife Linda has worshipped with our Orthodox friends in America, only to discover that the Orthodox churches had been doing this for centuries!

4. *We need to be culturally relevant, while maintaining our biblical foundations*

The timeless truths of the Gospel haven't changed. How we package them has! If we genuinely care about reaching the next generation then we must make our events accessible to them. Frankly, so much of what our churches have become comfortable with as the norm, is hopelessly out of touch with trends in society. The music is important! If we cling to outdated forms we will cease to communicate. This has had a dramatic effect on all aspects of our gatherings. The music may be rock based or techno-dance, using lots of record decks. Sometimes there is a strong Celtic flavour, and a great variety of percussion. The use of skilful lighting and video projection enhances it all. There will be a variety of spoken contributions, but we try to keep these brief, unless we are gathered for a specific teaching purpose. Even then, we make our teaching as interactive as possible. A lot of personal stories are used. Testimony has always been a prominent feature of great revivals and prayer courses through everything, individually, in small groups and corporately as well.

5. *We must make room for the Holy Spirit!*

So often our meetings and events are packed with a tightly structured programme that allows no opportunity for God to move. As the Jews at Nazareth impeded the powerful ministry of Jesus by their unbelief, so we have been guilty of making the Holy Spirit's work a supporting act, not the main attraction. As a preacher, I know this all too well. It's easy to hide behind preaching, monopolising the time, so that our words become pre-eminent, not His works! Fear often plays a large part in this. If this is going to change, like Peter in the Gospels, we must be prepared to step out of the boat and begin to walk in Jesus' miraculous dimension.

Joseph Garlington, who leads a dynamic multi-racial church in Pittsburgh, USA, challenged us at a recent Pioneer Event. Talking about healing, he said that as a church, they discovered that they were rarely praying for the sick! When healing became a priority in their ministry then miracles began to happen. Deliverance and healing were two thirds of Jesus' original commission to His disciples. For many of us, and for whatever reason, the expectation of God to move miraculously has almost disappeared. If we want healings we must pray for the sick and not allow disappointments and setbacks to discourage us.

These are just some of the principles that affected our thinking, and gradually, a major shift took place. The main meeting room at our church facility was proving inadequate, and so we moved more of our gatherings to The Worx. Here the environment was more conducive to the outworking of this vision. If I further describe just a sample of our meetings you will begin to catch the flavour of what is happening.

I have already described the mistake we made at a previous baptismal service. Not wishing to repeat this, we moved our next baptism up to The Worx, in spite of the simple logistical problem that we didn't have a baptistry there! This was not a deterrent to the team however. One night, the lads popped down to a local Indian Restaurant, where we had a close relationship with the proprietor Oliur and his staff. They borrowed a large green refuse bin and dragged it up to The Worx. There followed a valiant attempt to hose it down and get rid of all the curry smells and stains, and soon we had our first mobile baptistry! It was great because when we baptised one of the youth, James, we could wheel it right into the midst of everybody. He climbed up some steps to get in and after the baptism and prayer, we wheeled him out to the car park with hilarious shouts and cheers. The symbolism that a rubbish bin provided seemed to make it a highly appropriate vehicle for baptism in every way. You will be relieved to know that many baptisms later, a clean, 'Mark 2' refuse bin has been purchased from the council!

Over some months a series of 'Firestarters' events were

held on Saturday evenings at The Worx. The idea was to gather youth from churches around us and literally 'light a fire'. A tremendous amount of thought and planning went into these events as they were intended not simply to be a showcase for our own ideas, but to start a bush fire of the Holy Spirit across the region. Creative prayer and worship was always a primary focus.

On one of these evenings, tents were used as centres for prayer, each with a major theme: the family, the workplace, school and college etc. As people arrived in the car park outside the building, a tent had been erected with a burning brazier in the entrance. Here people received instruction for the evening and were then commissioned to go in groups down the High Street, praying outside strategic places – McDonalds, Pizza Hut, the cinema, a notorious pub, and so on. On returning to The Worx they found four main tents pitched inside the building, and the idea was to spend time at each of these specific prayer centres, praying for a variety of issues.

On this particular evening, a remarkable thing happened. One of our young guys, John Rouse, left the building after all the preparations had been finished to walk down to the High Street with a friend. The building was eerily quiet as they left, with subdued lighting and the tents assembled around the main hall. As they walked down the lane to the main road they found a man lying in the gutter and went to see if they could help him. John offered to go back to The Worx and get him a drink of water. When he entered the building he was gripped by an extraordinary atmosphere, and then noticed a brightness in one of the tents with two figures laughing and talking together. He said that these 'shining ones' were the most beautiful people he had ever seen, and was completely overawed. He withdrew from the building and returned to the man in the gutter only to discover that he had disappeared!

At this time John was not the 'full-on' Christian he is now, and this experience deeply impacted him. At Fire-starters he shared what had happened as the people assembled, and God's power came down. Someone was immediately healed, another converted and all kinds of responses broke out at the start of the evening.

On arriving at The Worx you never knew quite what to expect. It was refreshingly unpredictable! Often, there was a process of preparation which would take place outside or in the foyer of the building. We were frequently challenged as to whether we had clean hands and pure hearts to 'ascend the hill of the Lord' as in Psalm 24. Once inside, the emphasis was on engaging everyone in the focus for that evening, unless you genuinely wanted to 'opt out'. There was room for that as well! Several activities may be happening at once. On a large sheet of paper you wrote the names of people you were praying for in wallpaper paste, then threw handfuls of seed at them so that the names were now dramatically embossed. A human tunnel of prayer may be formed in another area while another group were anointing people with oil and praying for those who were sick. Suddenly, the pace would change. Everyone would come together to listen to a scripture, exhortation or engage in corporate worship. Then, maybe we would go back into groups again for prayer or the breaking of bread. Often, after an hour in a more traditional service, I find myself looking at my watch. In these gatherings, two to three hours could speed by without a yawn.

However, changing the tactics alone will not accomplish all we are longing for. We need a powerful team, one that can dismiss the opposition and create the winning plays. More than anything, a source of strength was unlocked at The Worx that has proved effective until this day.

Chapter 6

The Supporters Club

The process involved in changing the focus of New Generation Church required a huge paradigm shift for most of the members. This was not easily accomplished and involved a lot of adjustments and heartache, but it has been worth it all. Early on in the process, a passage of Scripture came alive to me as a prophetic description of what was to happen with us.

This passage in Genesis chapter 25 concerns the relationship between Abraham's son Isaac, and his wife Rebecca. She was barren, and having no children was an unpleasant stigma in her society. After many years of childlessness she and Isaac cried to the Lord in desperation, and miraculously, she conceived – in some ways not unlike Isaac's own conception. As the pregnancy developed, Rebecca began to feel increasingly uncomfortable as the twin babies 'jostled each other within her'. She inquired of the Lord as to the cause of this disturbance and received a remarkable prophetic word in response:

> 'Two Nations are in your womb, and two peoples from within you will be separated; one people will be stronger than the other, and the older will serve the younger.'
>
> (Genesis 25:23)

Long before scans and all the technology that accompanies modern pregnancy, she knew that she was to give birth to twin boys and that they were to be leaders in their own right – patriarchal heads of new nations. But the punch-line was this: **'The older shall serve the younger'**.

This latter statement encapsulates a key in the changes that have taken place with us. The whole story is very instructive for church leaders everywhere who are willing to respond to a fresh initiative from the Holy Spirit. As the drama unfolds, it moves from **barrenness**, to **conception**, followed by **internal conflict**, that eventually leads to **fruitfulness**. Many of us will recognise this process from our own experience. How many churches have struggled with the stigma of increasing barrenness. As the prophet Haggai said:

'You have planted much, but harvested little.'

(Haggai 1:6)

Our best efforts may have seen little fruit, often leaving the faithful discouraged and demoralised. However, when we cry out for change, for Divine intervention, we often get more than we bargained for! In Rebecca's womb a conflict was going on that was very uncomfortable for her – one that she didn't understand. In the womb of the Church worldwide a similar conflict is taking place. A different order is emerging and it takes courageous leaders to make way for what God wants to do. If we dig our heels in at this point; if we settle for compromise; if we say 'I don't want to rock the boat, I must keep the peace at all costs', then God will have to choose other people and some other situation in which to accomplish His purpose. What often happens at this point is that everything 'boils over', trauma ensues, and splits occur – often accelerated by the intransigence of older leaders on the one hand, and the impatience of the younger team on the other.

At one point in our development, to accommodate this conflict we divided our meetings. We set up Youth Church at The Worx, while the older end of our congregation carried on with a different style of gathering. The effects of this were very interesting. It soon became evident where the life in the church was! I am quite sure that if we hadn't made this move when we did, we would have lost a lot of our key young leaders, not because they were rebellious, but because they were increasingly stifled and frustrated. We usually met altogether at least once a month, and this was always encouraging, but more and more our older people were saying: 'We don't want to be left on the shelf – we want to be where the life is!'

As things have progressed, the lines have become increasingly blurred and a new unity is constantly emerging.

What does it mean for 'the older to serve the younger?' There are a number of practical ways in which we can help facilitate such a shift in the equilibrium:

1. Financially

Naturally, the 'mature' section of the church has resources that the younger ones don't. They have a more established lifestyle and are used to disciplined giving. But, instead of harbouring a resentful 'Why should we pay for all this?' attitude, a more positive approach would be: 'This is our future. What a privilege it is for us to be able to invest in it.'

2. Hospitality

Church at its best should represent an extended family. Many young people today come from a less than satisfactory home life. It's great when more mature Christians in the church are willing to open up their homes, share their family life, and give encouragement and wise council to young people – sometimes just a shoulder to cry on. Ray and Maddy are in their fifties and could really just sit back and take life easy. Instead, they constantly have people round their table, occupying spare beds or even the caravan in their back garden. So many detached young people at The Worx have seen them as a surrogate Mum and Dad. It's true they have special gifts, but such gifts only develop as you take the first simple steps – like having extra food ready at lunch or dinner, or filling empty seats in the car when you're going somewhere nice.

3. Mentoring

The ability to take someone 'under your wing' and be a mentor to them in terms of lifestyle, spiritual gifts and ministry is a great asset. Not everyone has the personality or ability to do this effectively, but many more could if they were prepared to make the effort. Even Jesus had to invite the twelve to follow Him; it didn't just happen!

Just imagine if everyone in the church was being effectively understudied. Just as in a theatre production all the principle characters must have an understudy so that the production doesn't come to a halt if someone has the flu, so all of us need to impart our wisdom and experience, our gifts and abilities, to younger men and women.

Looking at the outstanding leaders of the Old Testament, I have often thought that Moses did a very good job in preparing Joshua to take over his leadership. However, when Joshua comes to the end of his life, evidently no one had been prepared to assume his role. It's no wonder that the book of Judges, one of the most chaotic periods in Israel's history, follows on from the death of Joshua!

Serving as a leader

As you contemplate what it means for the older to serve the younger, all kinds of creative and practical responses may come to you, but within this, there is one foundational principle that unlocks everything: **he who serves, leads!**

In our present society, the whole idea of 'the ministry' has assumed a status that was never intended in the original word. When Jesus said:

> *'The son of man came not to be ministered to, but to minister and give his life as a ransom for many'*
> (Matthew 20:28)

He gave us the key to effective Christian ministry and indeed, any kind of leadership. One of the most powerful events in the Gospels is when Jesus washes His disciples' feet (John 13:1–17).

We need foot washing leadership! Only a person secure in who they are and what they are doing is capable of this! Just consider the number of times in this story that it says Jesus 'knew' what He was doing! In verse 3 it says:

> *'Jesus knew that the Father had put all things under his power, and that he had come from God and was returning to God.'*

And also, in verse 11:

> *'...he knew who was going to betray him...'*

It was out of this knowledge – this security in who He was, what He had come for, and where He was going – that He took the towel and washed His disciples feet. Identity precedes function! We have so many people in Christian ministry today whose identity is **in** their function. They cannot afford for their position or status to be threatened because that is who they are! When Jesus humbled Himself to fulfil the most menial, servant role, one that none of the disciples cared to do lest it threatened their position and put them at a disadvantage, He said to them:

> *'I have set you an example that you should do as I have done for you.'*   (John 13:15)

He never questioned the authenticity of His leadership. This kind of service was not an ingratiating thing, designed to curry favour with His disciples. In fact He said:

> *'You call me "Teacher", and "Lord" and rightly so, for that is what I am.'*   (John 13:13)

In all of this, Peter's reaction is interesting. Finally shamed, because Jesus was doing what he should have done without question, he makes a big show of Jesus not washing his feet. Jesus response to this is very dramatic:

> *'Unless I wash you, you have no part with me.'*
> (John 13:8)

The very essence of the Kingdom of God is about serving and being served. If we can't do either – if we must be the 'top dog' and have the 'last word' – if our position is all-important, then our leadership will always be flawed.

It's interesting that the whole drama of this leadership struggle was enacted in the context of a meal. Forget the platform – what are you like at home? It would be easy to spiritualise all this and take John chapter 13 out of context, which in our day could be translated, 'No one wants to do the washing up'!

So many of our church cultures have been riddled with male chauvinism, it's no wonder that we don't produce great leaders. Even familiar passages of Scripture such as Paul's advice on marriage in Ephesians chapter 5, have been loaded in favour of female servitude and male dominance. It has to be a very prejudiced interpreter that can only see wives submitting and husbands doing the loving. I can't tell you the number of homes I have stayed in where the husband is waited on hand and foot in the mistaken belief that this is the outworking of a biblical precedent. What I am saying here is that Jesus example of servant leadership does not require some lofty 'spiritual' response, but some earthy practicality. Those who are following us need to see that this is our lifestyle, not something we put on for special occasions.

As we embraced a new-style, younger leadership team for our church, it wasn't without cost to all of us who had previously carried responsibility. Others in our church could share very personally some of the pain of this transition. For Linda and me it was not so much a painful experience, because we were glad to see what was happening, but there were some very real challenges involved nonetheless.

I have always loved teaching and preaching, regarding both as very important elements in my particular set of gifts. In my developing years I was greatly influenced by leaders who thought nothing of speaking for at least an hour and quickly copied their longevity. As a student I began to preach in the small chapels around the Leicestershire countryside. One memorable night at a small Baptist church, I preached for an hour and a half from the book of Job. One older lady shook hands with me at the door as she left the service and said, 'Well, I'll remember to bring my sandwiches next time!'

Some years later I received an important prophecy: 'Let Peter's words be fewer, but with greater power.' Since that time I have paid careful attention to that word. A sure way to ruin a good meal is to eat too much. It can spoil everything that has gone before. How often our hopes have risen when a preacher has said the magic word 'finally', only for our expectations to be dashed by a succession of 'finally's' lasting another half an hour.

As our new style of church developed, I was sometimes not sure if there was a place for my kind of gift. I would occasionally be asked to speak, only to find my slot crammed in at the very end of a multifaceted programme. I also needed to learn how to bridge the cultural gap in my communications skills. Because of years of intensive Bible study, I was familiar with biblical idioms and illustrations that were like a foreign language to many of my hearers.

One lesson in communication was learnt while travelling among a remote Aboriginal tribe in Central Australia. Our friends, Ron and Sue Trudinger, had invited us to spend some time visiting the Pijinitjarra tribe from their mission base in Ernabella. Having driven several hours over a dirt road, we arrived at a tiny settlement in the heart of the Aboriginal lands. In the centre of the small town was a platform, a simple wooden stage, illuminated by two electric light bulbs. It was announced that I would speak from this platform to the community after nightfall. At first, it seemed that no-one would come, then shadowy figures appeared in the darkness and lit fires around the perimeter of the ground. There were lots of children and women wrapped in blankets, and men with eyes glowing in the light of their campfires. Wild dogs ran everywhere and insects constantly bombarded my face and neck as I stood under the light of a naked bulb.

I really gave it my best shot and preached a tried and tested message of Peter stepping out of the boat and walking on the water. I knew that Ron was an excellent interpreter, but he seemed to be taking his time with the translation. Later he explained to me that most of these people had never seen even a lake, let alone a boat! Apparently, both were in short supply in Central Australia.

One night in Sidcup, everyone laughed when I was talking about music and happened to mention the 'hit parade'! Of course, it's 'the charts' now, unless it's already called by a groovier name. I frequently struggled with the new style of music in the church, particularly the sound levels which were deafening at times. On other occasions the lights were so low that I couldn't read from my Bible, and I clearly remember the band who performed for a whole evening and I didn't hear a single lyric! No, I haven't sent for my pensioner's bus-pass just yet, but the culture shift was a real challenge to me.

The issue of finance was another sensitive area that had a profound impact on all of these changes. We had been fully supported by the church, and these days that's a heavy commitment, especially if you have children and a mortgage to sustain. As our team developed and my role changed, I knew that our support base needed to be adjusted. Younger team members deserved remuneration and it wasn't right for us to go on receiving the largest slice of the cake. I endeavoured to boost outside consultancy, but it wasn't easy. When we dropped a third of our salary to help this process, we really felt the pinch. We were not alone in this. Paul and Paula Weston, for example, made huge sacrifices. At the time when we wanted to increase Paul's salary, he refused to take it as he felt (rightly) that it would over-stretch the church's budget, and that others equally needed help. Ben Bullen, our school's evangelist, has worked for a fraction of the salary he could have commanded in the workplace. Chrissie Rogers, our administrator, has done the same, and we have a large pool of voluntary workers. For a long time Ben and Chrissie worked for no salary at all!

Make no mistake about it, this issue is often a key factor in the stranglehold that can develop around senior leadership, making radical changes in the team very difficult to achieve. Nor do I think that improved tithing and stewardship will resolve all of this. Too much money can disguise the real issues that could otherwise take place. Having said all of this, please be careful how you handle it. People's lives are at stake. There are faithful servants of God who have given their whole lives to the work of the Gospel, only to find themselves discarded when a new broom swept in. Churches have not been renowned for providing packages that included redundancy pay, medical benefits or a pension!

One untapped resource that can help many of our churches are older people who can take early retirement or planned redundancy, so that they can serve the church out of their lifetime of skills. This is an excellent way in which 'the older can serve the younger' and I think there's a lot of mileage in it. Another valuable resource is in those who succeed in their career or business to a point where they no longer need the large remuneration they are receiving. For such people to give themselves to the support of younger, emerging leaders is a wonderful thing, and a valuable investment for the future.

During the latter part of our time at New Generation Church, we were greatly helped by the prevailing attitude in our new team that made a peaceful transition possible. We were never made to feel unwanted, and I believe we made a valuable contribution to the life of the church until it was time for us to return to New Zealand. There was a supportive attitude throughout. Because of our relational building, difficulties were always talked out and not allowed to fester. Even at times when we unintentionally hurt one another, we sought quickly to find a place of forgiveness and reconciliation. I have been amazed to watch how skilfully the new team has managed to integrate old and young in the life of the church. The principle of sowing and reaping is particularly important at this crucial time of baton changing. If we sow an unthinking, arrogant attitude to those who are our predecessors, we shouldn't be surprised if this turns round and bites us at a later date.

Chapter 7

Substitutes

Since our return to New Zealand, Linda and I have had the satisfaction of watching the legendary national rugby team, the All Blacks, thrash two of their hottest opponents, the Wallabies from Australia, and the Springboks from South Africa. One controversial decision by the coaching staff has dominated media comment. Jonah Lomu, a fearsome winger with the extraordinary combination of massive build and speed, had spent the majority of these two important tests on the substitute bench. His cult status had not been enough to replace some of the new, emerging talent in the New Zealand back division. Watching his replacements play, I would have to agree with the coaches' decision at that time, though his form in the recent World Cup belied that decision.

Sir Alex Ferguson – probably one of the most successful soccer team managers of recent decades – released a fascinating autobiography, *Managing My Life*, in which he reveals just how difficult an issue this is, especially with a stable of top players.

When it comes to Christian leaders, making necessary changes to the 'team players' can be one of the most sensitive and difficult areas to handle. Not everyone has the grace to recognise when team changes are essential, and even when we are willing to face the facts, powerful emotions come into play.

I first came to terms with this in our emerging house church in Bristol during the early seventies. For some years I had loved to lead worship, especially from a piano. What I lacked in skill, I made up for with enthusiasm, and could always be relied upon to trot out a song! In our group was a young student, Peter Cutts, who enjoyed playing the guitar. At first, he was nervous to lead worship, but the more we encouraged him, the bolder he became. At the same time, certain things became clear to me. Of paramount importance was the need to make room for other gifts. The day of the all-singing, all-dancing, preaching, praying leader was fast coming to an end. We had to make room for the body to function. Coupled with this prior concern was the recognition that my abilities were severely limited. My style of playing was too dated, and my repertoire was similarly historic. I can still raise a laugh in any team meeting today by launching out in song with some golden oldie!

Of course, it wasn't so difficult for me, because I had other gifts that more than compensated for my demotion from the worship leading. What about the person for whom this is seemingly their primary contribution, and now it is being called into question?

Here then, is the 'Peter Principle' – something we learn from management studies. Simply put, this means to promote someone to their highest level of incompetence. Someone who is a great assistant manager one day, is promoted to become the main manager, only to discover that they have now been extended beyond the level of their gift. It happens all the time! The difficulty in church teams is that it is much easier to 'lay hands' on somebody than it is to reverse the process.

As we pursue this issue which dogs the progress of so many leadership teams, may I throw in a word of caution. Life is full of surprises! Sometimes, the people you least expect will make good, given the right encouragement and environment.

A perfect example of what I am referring to happened in our music group at Sidcup. Something we struggled with from the outset was a shortage of talented musicians. For a long time we had no drummer. Before we arrived at the church, a very talented drummer had left over some dispute and joined another congregation. A guy called Steve Chattaway had been observing this obvious need, and decided to pursue a practical solution. He went out and bought a set of drums and began to take lessons!

Before long, he began to arrive at church with his kit and was encouraged to 'have a go' – not by me I might add! I have to be really honest here. I didn't think Steve had it in him to be a drummer. His early outings on the skins were very painful for us all, and especially for him. People generally were not enthusiastic. I doubted if he had sufficient sense of rhythm to ever make a good drummer. Any musician will know how important this role is for 'driving' a band. From my perspective, we were headed for a serious 'pile-up' on the motorway!

It's at this point that I must eat humble pie! Steve has made it, and gets better every time I hear him play. Had we originally had some slick, over-subscribed, talented pool of musicians, he would probably have never had the chance. It says something for his commitment that he stayed with it, and the patience of Chris Lowth, leading the band at this time, and others, who encouraged him. The lesson is: a coach shouldn't make hasty substitutions. If Jesus had sacked the twelve for all the blunders they committed, none of them would have made it to the Day of Pentecost!

Another problem often found in church teams can be that of 'cronyism'. Simply put, this is the 'You scratch my back and I'll scratch yours' syndrome. Friendship, an important ingredient for team building, can sometimes get in the way of wise decisions. This is where an outside accountability can be helpful. It will greatly assist the health of the team if we don't hold everything 'in house'. To have input from outside of the church by trusted, mature ministries, will greatly enhance the building process, and help us sometimes to 'bite the bullet' in situations where we have procrastinated for far too long.

In John chapter 15, Jesus tackles the whole issue of fruitfulness in our lives. He says,

> *'You did not choose me, but I chose you and appointed you to go and bear fruit – fruit that will last.'*   (John 15:16)

There has sometimes been a conflicting attitude in peoples minds as to the nature of this fruit. It's rightly pointed out that, 'the fruit of the Spirit' outlined by Paul in Galatians is all about character (Galatians 5:22–23). So for some, to be fruitful, is to exhibit more and more of the character of Jesus in their lives. If this is the only thing that fruitfulness is about, we have a problem. I have known some very godly people who walk in personal holiness, but have no impact at all on the world around them. Fruitfulness in the Bible has equally to do with increase, as in the initial command to Adam and Eve in Genesis:

> *'Be fruitful and increase in number; fill the earth and subdue it.'*   (Genesis 1:28)

When a coach brings on other players, it is to produce the maximum effect in demolishing the opposition. We must always have that openness of spirit that is willing to look at our own lives and that of our team members, and ask the hard question: 'Just how effective are we?'

Jesus said:

> *'I am the true vine, and my Father is the gardener. He cuts off every branch in me that bears no fruit, while every branch that does bear fruit he prunes so that it will be even more fruitful.'*   (John 15:1–2)

The pruning process can seem ruthless to the person who doesn't understand the long-term goal! My father was not exactly renowned for his gardening skills, and the first time I saw him prune an apple tree in our garden I thought he had killed it, there was so little remaining of the original tree. However, the following season saw an excellent crop of apples, much to our surprise! If the pruning doesn't happen, the vine, tree, or rose bush, will get out of control, and the quality of the fruit and flowers will gradually deteriorate. Sometimes a branch will need to be 'cut off' because there is simply no fruitfulness and it is impeding the development of the rest of the vine. Even branches that are fruit bearing will need to be pruned to produce a better harvest.

Let me recommend to you a team exercise that can help in this process. This can be done 'one on one', but is especially helpful in a group situation where there is secure leadership. Ask the team to write careful answers to three questions:

1.   What are you currently doing?
2.   What would you like to be doing that you are not currently doing?
3.   What do you wish that you didn't have to do that is currently your responsibility?

You will then need to take time for each person to share what they have written. Help them with question one. People always leave out some crucial aspect of what they are doing and often these are time consuming matters. Listening to the answers as they are shared will give you a good overview of team members' areas of responsibility. You may immediately find some who are over-stretched and others who are under-used. When each person shares their response, ask the other team members to talk back frankly on each summary. This is the point at which it is very important to have secure and sensitive leadership steering such a discussion. We don't want people unnecessarily wounded, but we must have frank exchanges and appraisal of peoples gifts. So on question one, for example, are the other team members comfortable with what the person is doing? Are there area's where they will say, 'I'm not sure if this is the best use of your time. I think you should give yourself more to this instead'?

The second question, which highlights team members aspirations, is very important. We must know what people are thinking their future could be and determine if these aspirations are unrealistic or attainable – or if they need help to identify their true sphere of usefulness.

On question three, we must not immediately relieve a person of some more onerous responsibility. We all have to do things from time to time that we don't like. However, if a talented individual is bogged down with stuff they really don't enjoy all the time, it can stunt their effectiveness and cause them to look elsewhere. When someone is doing what they are supposed to be doing it just fits them like a comfortable sweater. When they are not in the right position there is something continually 'jarring' about it. The wheels don't turn smoothly.

When the Apostle Paul outlines some of the different gifts functioning within the church, and how they complement each other, he uses a very important phrase:

> *'Do not think of yourself more highly than you ought, but rather think of yourself with sober judgement, in accordance with the measure of faith God has given you.'*
>
> (Romans 12:3)

Every team member, including the Captain, needs to exercise 'sober judgement', and not think more highly of themselves than they should. We need a realistic appraisal that is not hampered by false modesty in the guise of spirituality.

In 1999, Manchester United Football Club achieved the coveted 'triple'. They won the FA Cup, the Premiere Division of the soccer league, and the European Cup Winners cup. The elusive 'triple' was accomplished with an unbelievable finish in injury time when a substitute scored in the closing moments of the game, then set up a second last minute goal. Anyone watching their progress during this awesome season will have been struck by one thing. Apart from the team on the field, at any one time the substitute bench contained a whole string of world-class players. Although financial strength has meant that they could regularly buy outstanding players in the transfer market, part of their strategy has been to build a stable of younger players, identified by their scouts, and to patiently invest a lot of time in the development of this new talent.

Everything that I am saying here assumes that we are bringing on potential substitutes. The goal set out so clearly in the New Testament is the release of everyone to realise their full potential. When Paul talks about specially gifted people in Ephesians chapter 4 – Apostles, Prophets, Evangelists, Pastors and Teachers – the main purpose of their giftedness is that it should be deployed in releasing others! That is,

> '... to prepare God's people for works of service, so that the body of Christ may be built up...'   (Ephesians 4:12)

This is not to suggest that we will no longer need any specially gifted players! The whole of society, not just the Church, is crying out for anointed leadership. This is why Paul encourages his protégé Timothy to impart his gift to others:

> 'The things you have heard me say ... entrust to reliable men who will also be qualified to teach others.'
>
> (2 Timothy 2:2)

In other words, Paul mentored Timothy who must now do the same for others in the expectation that they will reproduce themselves as well.

A healthy church will start with the young in this process. Samuel was a boy when he began to receive the word of the Lord for his spiritual father and for the nation of Israel. Some years ago our church in Bristol began to actively encourage the children to function in spiritual gifts. During one public meeting, Linda and I received a very important personal word of prophecy from an eight-year-old boy. In the same church, Neil and Zoe Edbrooke had their son Joshua playing the drums confidently with the worship band when he was so small you could scarcely see his head above the kit! Paul and Paula Weston and their team have constantly encouraged children and young people to be part of the action. When they travel out from the church, they invariably take younger people with them and encourage them to participate, not just go along for the ride.

This kind of environment can only be created where established leaders do not see emerging gifts as a perpetual threat. We need a 'make room mentality'. A story that graphically portrays this in the Old Testament concerns Abraham's son, Isaac. As he prospers in the Promised Land he comes into conflict with Abimelech, King of the Philistines, to the point where he is asked to move away. Abimelech said to Isaac,

> *'Move away from us; you have become too powerful for us.'*
> (Genesis 26:16)

Isaac moves with all his extended family, flocks and herds to the Valley of Gerar. A water supply is essential, so they begin to open up wells that had been deliberately blocked by the Philistines during Abraham's time, a common strategy in guerrilla warfare. When the fresh water starts to flow again at Gerar, the local herdsmen quarrel with Isaac's family, saying that the water belongs to them. Isaac calls this well 'Esek' which means 'dispute', and he has to move again. The next location proves to be no better as the same thing happens once more. Isaac opens the well and its ownership is then contested by the locals. He calls this one 'Sitnah', meaning 'opposition', as they make it impossible for him to stay there. Finally, Isaac and his family open a well that nobody contests and they call this 'Rehoboth', which means 'room'.

> *'Now the LORD has given us room and we will flourish in the land.'* (Genesis 26:22)

Reading this story we can so readily equate it with many of the power struggles in the Church today. You don't have to be very long around a church to discover if there is a 'make room' attitude emanating from the leadership. I'm not suggesting that church government should be a kind of free-for-all, but there are very powerful possessive and controlling spirits in many situations that make conflict inevitable. The actual words 'You have become too power-ful for us; move away' may not be verbalised, but effectively, that is the attitude that is being conveyed. Then, some well is unblocked that has lain dormant for a long time, and suddenly it becomes 'our water'!

Just consider the parochial spirits that come into play when a new church starts up. Sometimes this can be handled unwisely, without any reference to other Chris-tians already working in that location, but at the end of the day, we want to see the nations seeded with new churches; there's plenty of room!

Any church that is going to have a substitutes bench packed with potential players must have a non-threatened leadership at its core. It has to be 'His church' not 'our church' or worse, 'my church'. The measure we give will be the measure we receive, and still more will be added to us (Mark 4:24), but if we erect a tight fence around what we are doing, we'll lose it all in the long run.

Chapter 8

The Strip

There's been a lot of controversy in recent years surrounding the frequency with which top soccer football teams change their strip (uniform for US readers). It's been an economic ploy that has infuriated many of the nation's parents! Mum and Dad save hard for Christmas to buy little Johnny the latest rig of his favourite team, and it's a big hit at the cash register. They swallow hard and bite the bullet because they know a cheaper alternative won't do! Sometimes there's more than one outfit to buy. These days it could be equally important for little Jenny, besotted with the star player, and even Dad, well into his mid-life crisis, could want one as well! This plan is assured of success on Christmas morning, but then the marketing Guru's at club headquarters cunningly re-style the strip early in the New Year! The luckless family are already struggling with the credit card bill from the last lot!

So what does this have to do with reaching and releasing the next generation? Rightly or wrongly, image is very important in today's world. Look at an old photograph of your favourite team – the big baggy shorts and cumbersome boots. It all seems very quaint now! The trouble is that today's Church can often seem very quaint too, and totally irrelevant. This wouldn't be so bad if the world at large didn't reject the message as well as the institution because we insisted on being different!

Why have Christians won all the awards for being 'naff' and lacking the street-cred to communicate with today's culture? I know that we live in an image-obsessed society, and every kind of pitfall is out there for people who lack discernment, but as always, the Church has majored on the minors and passed up enormous opportunities to reach the next generation because of our insistence on clinging to dubious principles.

I love the stories of the great Missionary Pioneers. When Hudson Taylor decided to don Chinese gear and eat Chinese food, this was seen as an important radical move to reach a different culture. Is it any different for us to want to remove unnecessary obstacles from our lifestyle if we are going to reach today's world?

I'll never forget the first time we saw 'The Worldwide Message Tribe' in action. Linda and I were at the large camp conference, Spring Harvest, where I was a member of the speaking team. I had booked 'The Tribe' for a gig at a big Pioneer event later that year, and so we thought it would be good to meet them and see what they did. As we queued around the theatre with hundreds of teenagers, we did feel a little bit out of place. When we finally got inside and sat down in a row of seats, it was noticeable that no-one sat with us. The theatre was jammed, but we were on our own. Just before the show started, a very nervous looking lady arrived with her son, who was probably thirteen, and sat beside us.

The first hint that this would be different was a warning flashed on screen that the strobe lights could damage your health. Linda said, 'I think it's going to be loud'. Then the sound kicked in and 'The Tribe' exploded on stage. I think the lady sitting by us dragged her son out in the first two minutes. From then on, we never sat down again. It was electrifying! 'Jumping in the house, in the house, in the house, jumping in the house of God ...!' The dancers were fantastic; the costumes outrageous; Cameron Dante back-flipped his way across the stage. The kids loved it and all the way through the good news of the Gospel was proclaimed in a way that these young people could access. No wonder

'The Tribe' are reaching thousands of young people across their home city of Manchester. Along with Mike Pilavachi and the Soul Survivor Team, they have recently invaded the streets of Manchester for two weeks with an army of thousands of young people wanting to reach their culture to devastating effect.

While bands like 'The Tribe' and 'Delirious' are reaching their culture, not all Christians are happy with this. For many years I travelled in Scandinavia, particularly Norway, as an itinerant evangelist. I frequently visited a town on the west coast where God gave me a tremendous door of opportunity, especially as this town was an important College centre. On one visit, even with language difficulties, I sensed that something was wrong! I got my friend and interpreter, Tore Lende, to enquire what was going on and was astounded by his discovery. The elders of the sponsoring church were unhappy with me. Apparently, I wasn't wearing a dark suit and my hair was now too long! The presiding elder told me in all seriousness that people in the town would not be able to receive the Gospel I preached, because of how I looked! That very night I was asked to speak at a huge music festival in the College Gymnasium. Of the hundreds of young people packed into the hall, my hair was the shortest and my clothes far more conservative!

Why do Christians adopt attitudes like this? If you think that this is an isolated example, travel in the Bible-belt churches of the United States, where the dress code is often tighter than that of IBM! I was raised this way. When all the kids wanted tight trousers, my mother insisted I have wide flares. It was so embarrassing! When I got my trousers, I had to wait a week, then surreptitiously visit a tailor in the High Street to get them altered. Nowadays, kids want the baggiest pants available and the shortest haircut, and no doubt many a Christian parent is throwing a fit about that. Body piercing and tattoos have introduced a whole new raft of problems. It gets even more complicated if the young people start reading the Bible and discover that many of the Jewish women wore nose rings!

Apart from cultural conservatism, there is in my view, a prevailing attitude in Christian society rooted in a misguided view of biblical holiness. In its extreme forms, it leads to groups like the Amish community that we visited recently in Pennsylvania. Their transport is confined to horse-drawn traps and their clothing from another century. Television and radio is forbidden, and in many cases, electricity also. The whole of life is deliberately seen as a separation from the world to avoid contamination. Most Christians would not be as extreme as this, but often foster attitudes that are not dissimilar. I believe that there are three primary reasons for this: a misunderstanding as to the true nature of holiness; coupled with a flawed theology, and finally, fear.

True holiness

I was greatly helped by the comments of Bishop Trevor Huddlestone in the early seventies. We were both participating at a meeting in Central London that was challenging the moral decline in our society. The Bishop said: 'True holiness is wholeness. It's being made whole in the image of God.'

I have always thought Christians I met who talked about holiness as being a bit odd! In fact some of them were, with their uncut hair, make-up-less faces and embargoes on most pleasurable activities! I suppose I had encountered an aberration of true holiness, not the 'wholesomeness' that God had intended. I began to read the New Testament from this fresh perspective. A very powerful passage from the Apostle Peter took on a fresh meaning:

> 'His divine power has given us everything we need for life and godliness...' (2 Peter 1:3).

I had got the impression that these two qualities were mutually exclusive – life and godliness. You could hardly enjoy life and be godly at the same time! Now I began to realise that this is what the power of the Gospel was designed to achieve in us all. Peter goes on to say that:

> *'... he has given us his very great and precious promises, so that through them you may participate in the divine nature and escape the corruption in the world caused by evil desires.'* (2 Peter 1:4)

I originally thought that this meant 'escape from the world' which is what I'm sure the Amish are trying to do. I hadn't realised that it is the corruption itself, not the world, that we must avoid. The world is God's world! My body is God's body! It doesn't really belong to the devil – he's an illegal squatter! If the world is such a bad place, then Jesus set us a pretty poor example, because He seemed very much at home in it and made friends with lots of sinners.

Another passage, often thundered from pulpits, is Romans 12:1–2. When Paul urges us to present our bodies to God and not to conform to the world, it's easy to approach this from a very negative perspective. I heard a lot of people talk about 'not conforming' when I was a young man. Not many talked about being transformed which is at the heart of this message. Being transformed and becoming a trans-former gave me a whole new slant on life and the possibility of healing the sickness in our society with God's wholeness!

True theology

Not only is there a very negative presentation of holiness in many evangelistic and charismatic churches, but almost an extreme pessimism concerning human nature. Dr Jeff Simmonds, of the Bible College of New Zealand, has written an excellent article in *Reality* magazine examining the theology of Eastern Orthodoxy. He says:

> 'We inherit from Augustine a particular interpretation of the Fall, a doctrine reaffirmed by the Reformers, of

the total depravity of humanity, and a negative attitude to all things sexual ... Augustine and Calvin both taught that humans are incapable of good desires and that humans lack freedom not to sin. Orthodoxy, however, recognises that God did not take away free will from humanity after the Fall, and therefore that all of us have the ability to choose good ... Orthodoxy, takes much more seriously than the West, the biblical teaching that we are made in the image of God – we are, all of us, "icons" of God: we bear his image within us.'   (*Reality* Magazine, Issue 33, June/July 1999)

I must confess, I am not a Calvinist! As a young Christian I had a brush with Calvinism that almost successfully dampened my evangelistic passion. A fine Bible teacher, Roger Forster, helped me re-think my faith at this critical time, and I re-shaped my thinking in terms of what I now believe is a more biblical world view. That the image of God in man has been marred because of sin is without question, but to suggest that mankind is totally depraved is manifestly not true. Just think of the people you know for starters.

Why is this important? Because so much of the creativity that we see even in this fallen world is evidence of the Creator's stamp upon humanity. The way we view our fellow human beings will inevitably affect how we treat them. It will greatly influence the vibe we give off and our ability to draw from their creative energy as well. Had we been involved in the encounter Jesus had with the woman of Samaria in John chapter 4, there might have been an entirely different outcome! Many of us would not have spoken to her in the first place. Had we done so, it would probably have come across as patronising and condescending. Would we have dared to tackle the deeply theological issues that Jesus broached with this evidently immoral woman? Could we have spoken at all without heaping judgement and condemnation on her? Would we have coped with the censorious attitude of the disciples on their return? Jesus, however, saw the potential in this tragic life, and in winning her, won her whole community as well.

True faith

The bottom line for so many Christians, especially those of us who are older, is fear. The reason so many parents get up-tight about their children's behaviour is because they remember what they were like at their age! My parents came from good Victorian stock and never breathed a word about sex. The only word my mother ever spoke to me on the subject came at a time when she suspected (correctly), that I had been masturbating. Full of fear, she said: 'You mustn't touch that!' I guess this has been the attitude of the Church to sex all along, which is why there is often very little helpful teaching and counsel when it is most needed.

Fear has governed so much of our interaction with society. If we emphasise **grace** – so central to New Testa-ment teaching – perhaps everyone will take advantage of it and end up in sin. If we allow **that** kind of music, standards will be eroded. If they dress like **that**, everyone will be seduced. The list is never-ending. I once helped a sweet old lady get free from a lifetime of pain and guilt. She had been raised in a very legalistic Holiness Church, known as 'the black stocking' church because of the long black clothes they had to wear. This church had been riddled with all kinds of moral corruption, and as a young woman, she had been badly abused. The notion that strict dress codes would avert sexual misconduct was completely naïve.

I'm convinced that the only antidote for such intimidat-ing fear is to build true faith into people:

> '...*perfect love drives out fear.*'   (1 John 4:18)

The reality of Christ's divinity must be matched by His attractive, wholesome, humanity. Some years ago I was hosting a seminar for church leaders in Christchurch, New Zealand. A vicar from a local Parish Church made a memorable contribution. Speaking in beautiful Oxford English, he explained how he had recently had some conflict with the Parish Council. They had passed a petition asking everyone to oppose the practice of topless sunbathing on Brighton Beach in Christchurch. He said, 'I told them I didn't feel free to sign it, as I had been a missionary for many years in Papua New Guinea, and frankly, many of my congregation were topless and bottomless as well!'

Not only does perfect love cast out fear, it covers a multitude of sins as well (1 Peter 4:8).

To cross the cultural gaps and reach the emerging generations we need to be saturated in God's love. We need faith that tackles the real issues and refuses to get side-tracked. A well known international Bible teacher, for whom I have the profoundest admiration, recently sent out one of his regular 'Update tapes' to his supporters. Commenting on his concern over the use of Rock Music in church services he expressed the lack of peace he felt in his spirit, adding, 'I know where this comes from – Pagan Africa!'

Apart from the cultural slight, this underscores what I am trying to say. It's a cultural conflict, not a spiritual one. The greatest streams of gospel music in the world have come out of 'Pagan Africa'. We mustn't allow our personal preferences to suddenly become a spiritual standard for everyone else.

I was with another great Bible teacher some years ago at a national conference in England. It was at the time when we were seeking to encourage dance as a legitimate form of worship, and this man was evidently feeling uncomfortable with it. A young woman, very gifted in dance, was enhancing the worship with her creative gifts when she accidentally backed into the tent pole of the large marquee we were meeting in. This confirmed all this man's suspicions. He told me afterwards that this was evidence to him that God was not in the dance! I wondered in the light of this how many anointed preachers who had tripped on the platform or knocked over a glass of water, dropped their notes, left their flies undone, or faced any of the other hazards confronting preachers, would have their ministry similarly disqualified!

The problem is that these were both fine men who have had tremendous influence in the Church world-wide. One word from them would effectively disqualify vast areas of creative ministry. What began as a cultural preference, is now endorsed with spiritual authority and the Church takes another step backwards in terms of its contemporary relevance.

We need a new strip, a new uniform. David couldn't take on Goliath in Saul's armour and we can't afford to be weighed down by the restraints of a previous style, a past anointing, whatever you like to call it. There will be plenty of 'brothers' who will resent our getting involved at all and Goliath will do his best to ridicule our efforts. He's in for a nasty shock!

Chapter 9

Training

Throughout this book, I have freely used sporting metaphors. The Apostle Paul was obviously familiar with the Greek Games, perhaps even a fan himself! Several references suggest this, but one passage is so graphic that I have included it all:

> 'Do you not know that in a race all the runners run, but only one gets the prize? Run in such a way as to get the prize. Everyone who competes in the games goes into strict training. They do it to get a crown that will not last; but we do it to get a crown that will last for ever. Therefore I do not run like a man running aimlessly; I do not fight like a man beating the air. No, I beat my body and make it my slave so that after I have preached to others, I myself will not be disqualified for the prize.'   (1 Corinthians 9:24–27)

Here we have a challenge to be competitive and not to be afraid of discipline and training. Paul's life had the specific focus of a champion athlete, and he was determined to cross the finishing line first and get the prize. To this end, he enslaved his body so that he could fulfil the call of God on his life. Unless we have a similar focus and discipline, and are willing to be 'in training', it's unlikely that we'll fulfil our greatest ambitions.

As we near the end of the first year of the new millennium we face some exceptional challenges. There is a temptation to over-indulge on every hand. The consumption of unhealthy fast food is rocketing. More and more young people spend hours each day glued to a TV, video-screen or computer monitor. There is less participation in healthy physical activity as we increasingly become spectators. Destructive habits involving drugs, alcohol and tobacco are at epidemic proportions. The abuse of our bodies through sexual promiscuity is now virtually taken for granted everywhere. All of it costs money, and the credit card culture says: 'Live now, pay later.'

No doubt the first century AD carried its own set of temptations, so that Paul needed to say to his young protégé, Timothy:

> '... *train yourself to be godly. For physical training is of some value, but godliness has value for all things, holding promise for the present life and the life to come.*'
> (1 Timothy 4:7–8)

As a student, I lived for three years among top athletes and sportsmen who took their training very seriously. They knew that if they didn't, there was always someone else waiting in the wings ready to oust them. It was around this time that God got hold of my life and I started thinking differently about my future. If my friends could train so rigorously for a brief moment of glory on an athletics track or a football field, was I prepared to train for the eternal rewards of Christ and His Kingdom?

You cannot separate the word disciple from the word discipline. Alone, I saturated myself in the Scriptures and prayer with a determination to be more like Jesus. In public, I looked for people whose lives I wanted to emulate and did everything I could to learn from them. Paul twice commanded the Corinthian church to imitate him (1 Corinthians 4:16; 11:1), and sent his own 'son' Timothy on a visit to them to make sure that they knew what this meant (1 Timothy 4:17).

As we confront the issue of discipline and enlist the help

of the Holy Spirit to get into serious training, it will mean different things for each one of us. The first real challenge for me was to get to grips with the Bible. I had a Sunday School knowledge of the Bible and was currently involved with some theological study, all of which came from a very destructive liberal perspective. I discovered that the Bible was a dead book to those who are spiritually dead. One immediate result of my conversion was that the Bible came alive to me. I became desperately hungry for God's Word. To satisfy this hunger I determined to read through the whole Bible in one year. In fact I read the Old Testament once and the new Testament twice during that first year at a time when I was studying for my final examinations. I remember praying: 'Lord, I will seek first Your Kingdom and Your righteousness, if You will help me fulfil my other study obligations as well.'

This plan worked really well and put me in a strong position for my future vocation. I was so encouraged by the impact of Scripture on me that the following year I read the Old Testament twice and the New Testament four times, just as my basic reading – a pattern I followed for many years after that. I can't begin to tell you what an important aspect of training this has been for my life. God's Word has truly been for me, '...*a lamp to my feet and a light for my path'* (Psalm 119:105).

Not only have I received constant spiritual guidance and nourishment for my own soul, but I've been able to share the Scriptures effectively with thousands of people around the world.

Another crucial aspect of training for me was the disciplining of my emotions and affections. I knew that if I wanted to make spiritual progress, I had to put a stop to casual relationships with a steady stream of girlfriends. But for some radical surgery in this area of my life, I'm sure that I would have missed the fantastic plan God had for me. At the time, this discipline seemed particularly painful, but it enabled me to give single-minded attention to my spiritual growth. When, after several single years, Linda came into my life, it was with an overwhelming assurance that here was God's perfect provision of a partner for me. I'm so glad that I had stopped 'playing the field'! I could have messed up big time!

Training involved disciplined use of time. I began to value the early morning hours when I could seek after God without interruption. I became much more careful as to how I used my time and tried to avoid getting to bed too late so that I was wiped out for the next morning. This will differ from person to person and during the different seasons in life. You must find what works for you.

At one time, I laid down my position in a local rugby team so that I could devote more time to visitation on a very needy council housing estate. Again, this was an important personal choice, not a prescription for everyone else.

More than anything, I disciplined myself to pray. Paul's advice to the Ephesians to *'pray in the Spirit on all occasions with all kinds of prayers and requests'* (Ephesians 6:18) became very important to me. When I secured my first teaching job in Bristol I took this very seriously. I would rise at 5.30am in the morning so that I could spend an hour in prayer and Scripture reading before leaving for work. My drive to work was at least half an hour through very busy traffic, so I learned to pray as I travelled, making the most of the time. Often, during lunchtime at school, I would drive up to the top of a steep hill that overlooked the city, so that I could engage in further intercession. The drive home after work was similarly interspersed with prayer and praise. Often the evenings would find me further engaged in prayer-centred activities. It was a very intense time of training for me and I have been reaping the spiritual benefits of this work-out ever since!

An aspect of Paul Weston's leadership at The Worx that has delighted me has been the increasing priority that has been given to prayer. Although The Worx began as a youth drop-in, it has become increasingly a centre for prayer! This shouldn't surprise us. Getting seriously involved in the

Youth Culture made us realise we were in a mega battle-zone. You can't afford to have untrained soldiers there! Some of David's 'Warfare Psalms' took on fresh meaning!

> *'He trains my hands for battle.'*   (Psalm 18:34)

> *'Praise be to the Lord my rock, who trains my hands for war, my fingers for battle.'*   (Psalm 144:1)

Everyone knows the armour passage in Ephesians chapter 6 where Paul tells us we are not fighting flesh and blood, as David was, but powerful spiritual enemies. Paul Weston has really got hold of this and has been constantly training the church in prayer.

During prolonged periods the church has met at The Worx to pray four nights a week at 10.00pm. Sometimes, the meetings will last for an hour, often they carry on much later. One night, after a long session, one of the teenagers was walking home down Sidcup Hill at one o'clock in the morning. A police car pulled over to enquire what he was doing. When he explained that he had been at a prayer meeting at The Worx it was readily accepted by two incredulous policemen. They had to get used to unlikely characters coming from the place of prayer!

Different people are encouraged to lead these prayer times, making them as creative and interactive as possible. I remember one evening when Martin James had set up 'the walls of Jericho'. This had been done by wrapping large rolls of paper round the main pillars of the building. After a biblical exhortation from the story in Joshua chapter 6, we repeatedly marched around these walls in prayer, taking hold of all kinds of issues inspired by the Holy Spirit, until we finally shouted and broke the walls down. As I recall it, someone dived right through the wall and collapsed on the floor.

I've no doubt in my mind that prayer has been an important key to so much that has happened in Sidcup. Sometimes our prayer-room at The Worx would be packed with people and then at other times there may only be ten or a dozen people present. Often, it would be very loud, full of high praise and worship, with much corporate declaration, then at other times, it would be very still and personal. Sometimes we would be engaged with national or international issues; another evening we might focus on a local need or pray for specific individuals. The laying on of hands, anointing with oil and breaking bread have all taken on fresh significance during these times.

While the prayer room has had a special focus for these gatherings, sometimes we would move out into the whole building, or move outside altogether to pray in specific locations in the town or prayer-walk the streets. All of it has been a learning process in which we encourage one another to take fresh steps of faith. One of the lessons we have been learning is to stay with an issue until we achieve a breakthrough. We are often in too much of a hurry, anxious to move on, when God actually wants us to prevail over a particular matter.

Some years ago in our church in Bristol we learnt an important lesson. We had gathered in a central city church for a night of celebration and had a guest speaker present from New Zealand. Scarcely had the evening begun when one of the young men arrived with alarming news. The baby daughter of one of our key leadership couples, Nic and Jenny Harding, had been rushed into intensive care with suspected meningitis. Nic is a doctor and fully understood the serious implications of her condition. The congregation was stunned! Prayer was offered for the little girl and her family and then the worship leader introduced another song and the meeting got under way in a very subdued fashion.

In my heart I knew that we were about to miss the issue in hand so I stepped in. I drew the attention of the congregation back to the news that was troubling all our minds – Nic and Jenny's daughter – and we went to war! We used a song of Dale Garratt's that is still one of the most powerful that I know in this context:

'Summon your power O God,
Show us you strength as you have done before.'

These are words from Psalm 68, one of David's 'warfare'
psalms. Dale had set these words to a powerful melody
accompanied by a warfare drum beat.

'The chariots of God are tens of thousands,
and thousands of thousands;
arise O Lord and speak the word,
and all your enemies will scatter.
A sound of joy will soon be heard,
a shout, your warriors will answer.'

That night we took this song and would not let it go! We
stayed with it until faith was born in our hearts, so that
when we shouted, this particular wall of Jericho would
come crashing down! And it did! Nothing much else
happened that night, I think the guest speaker got ten
minutes at the end, but in that intensive care unit, Nic and
Jenny's baby was healed.

Why are we always in such a hurry to move on? I often
say to worship leaders, 'Find out what the Holy Spirit is
singing and stay with it. Come back to it again and again if
necessary.'

To speakers, including myself, I often say, 'Be prepared
to abandon the message you have prepared, and sometimes
be willing not to speak at all if God is doing something
else.'

One time in Kentucky, an unusual prophet, Hal Stenson,
who had never met me before, gave me a very direct word of
prophecy, part of which had to do with my ministry. He
said, 'The Holy Spirit is saying – close the book!'

I Immediately knew what he was saying. All my life I had
been 'opening the book' to people, and important as this is,
I needed to leave my comfort zone where I felt safe, and
begin to bring fresh dimensions of the Holy Spirit's ministry
to people. Like Jesus in the Synagogue at Nazareth, there

was a moment to roll up the scroll of Scripture and bring God's immediate word to the people (Luke 4:14–30).

As the prayer strategy at The Worx developed, Paul felt that the Holy Spirit was calling us to an even deeper intensity of prayer. A turning point was a special month of 'intimacy' which took place through October 1998 and had a dramatic affect on the life of the church. During this month, several meetings a day were planned in which we could come near to God so that He would come near to us! (James 4:8). Apart from private prayer, a small group would meet to pray early in the morning. Another meeting was planned at lunchtime, perhaps with Team or family members at home, then a further session followed after school, often including children and young people. Prayer at night would happen around 8.00pm or 9.00pm, usually for six days each week. If visiting musicians or other ministries came, they were invited to flow with us in the intimacy process, capturing the prophetic spirit of the time. Many did, often being as blessed themselves as they imparted blessing to others.

Seeking God together has a way of dealing with so many obstacles and preparing the way for the Holy Spirit to move. Lots of stories have come out of this time, but one is my favourite. Towards the end of the month, Chilean Apostle, Miguel Escobar, came for a weekend of ministry. Many dramatic things happened, but one evening as he was feeling extremely tired, Miguel asked to go home early, encouraging Paul to pray with people who had responded to his message. At the start of the evening, Paul had welcomed visitors and assumed that one of these, Mary, a sixth former from a local school, was a Christian visiting from another church. When he went to pray for some thirty people standing in the front, he announced that Mary would help him do the praying. At this point, Chris Lowth, who had brought her to the meeting, said in a stage whisper: 'She's our baby-sitter, not yet a Christian, and this is her first time at such a meeting.'

Paul was somewhat thrown by this, but felt to carry on.

As they prayed for the first person, the Holy Spirit powerfully fell on them to Mary's great surprise. She said. 'Is this a
charismatic church? I've heard about this! I've been writing
a paper at school about speaking in tongues and have never
seen this before!'

Needless to say, she was soon radically converted and the
Holy Spirit has been using her since that time. This particular incident serves to underline a principle that has become
very important to us:

Many people need to **belong** before they **believe**!

The church needs to be a welcoming place where people
feel accepted, not ostracised. In the early chapters of Acts,
the dynamic of community was so strong that it was itself
an attractive and infectious thing. Evangelism was not
contrived or artificial, it was the natural overflow of a
shared life, an incredible sense of belonging. Undergirding
all the evangelism of the New Testament is this sense of
community. There is a place for the anointed evangelist to
speak to a vast crowd as Peter did on the Day of Pentecost.
Even then it specifically records that *'Peter stood up with the
eleven . . . '* (Acts 2:14), not in isolation. The three thousand
that responded to his message by public baptism, were
immediately added to the community of believers, not left
to go it alone. In The Worx this will mean joining a specific
youth cell where a lot of the foundational training we have
referred to goes on. This is a small group context designed
to encourage personal development. In Chapter 10 I
describe a more specific leadership training forum called
'Essence'.

Training does not just happen, it must be planned and
provoked. One of our team, Kevin Carvosso, is a personal
fitness trainer. His extraordinary claim to fame in the life of
the church was a time when the Holy Spirit came upon him
and he could only walk backwards! This strange occurrence
happened during one of our nightly prayer meetings and
gave his father quite a shock when he arrived home. He

found it particularly difficult when he tried to negotiate the stairs and was thankful to fall into bed. However, the next morning having forgotten about the incident, he was very shocked to discover that he still couldn't walk forward. It was highly embarrassing to have to ring his employer to explain why he could not come to work!

For nearly three days this strange manifestation persisted. Kevin realised that God was trying to get his attention over some issues in his life. We were all relieved when he finally broke through. One spin off from this bizarre time were some exceptional opportunities to share the gospel with his colleagues at work. Most of the time though, Kevin is moving forward, often very energetically.

For some years, Linda and I have been concerned about our overall health and fitness – part of our training for God's call on our lives. We had diligently disciplined our eating habits and planned frequent exercise, often combining prayer and walking. During our last two years at Sidcup, Kevin developed some of his personal training skills on us as the geriatric Guinea Pigs! His varied pace relays around the park and programmed exercises were a great help to us, and the regularity of the sessions helped us in maintaining focus. It was always a fun-filled, exhilarating time. He often provoked our competitive spirit and delighted in making a spectacle of us to the many dog walkers and groups of school children. Having moved to the other side of the world we no longer have the benefit of Kevin's sessions, but we do have the Holy Spirit! I often say to people, 'You have the greatest personal trainer in the world at your disposal twenty four hours a day.'

Jesus promised His disciples, who were troubled by the fact that He was going to leave them, that the Holy Spirit would be everything to them individually that He had been. He said,

> '... *You know him, for he lives with you and will be in you. I will not leave you as orphans; I will come to you.*'
>
> (John 14:17–18)

Chapter 10

Penalty

'God forgives even David Beckham', shouted the poster outside an enterprising church in Britain's soccer heartland. England's chances of winning the 1998 World Cup in France had been torpedoed by the unfortunate sending off of their Manchester United super-star in the second round match with Argentina. A foolish and blatant flick of Beckham's boot at Diego Simeone, meant the end of England's World Cup hopes, and inspired a vicious and relentless hounding of the player by the media and public alike when he returned to Britain. His Manchester United boss, Alex Ferguson, said of this unfortunate episode: 'He could hardly have been more vilified if he had committed murder or high treason.'

The flip-side of success on the field of sport is failure, and when this failure is accompanied by an element of disgrace, such as a positive drug test on an Olympic Athlete, the consequences can be devastating.

When it comes to the development of new leadership teams in the life of the Church, one of the hardest things to handle is discipline and the judgements that will inevitably be required from time to time, in order to maintain a healthy moral and spiritual ethos in everything that we build. It can be extremely traumatic when a player has to be penalised, either temporarily or more permanently, because of their conduct. I want to focus in this chapter, therefore, on the issue of discipline and present some clear guidelines that will hopefully prevent leadership teams from being derailed.

The New Testament does provide us with some clear guide lines on these issues, but all too often, these are not clearly adhered to, either because of ignorance, or an unwillingness to take the responsibility required of us as leaders. In the 'good cop, bad cop' interrogation scenario in detective movies, we would all like to be the good guy!

Before outlining the biblical principles involved in church discipline, let me refer to an incident that catalysed my own need to be pro-active in this area. At the beginning of my ministry in the mid-sixties, I was a teaching Elder in a growing new church. We had a young man involved as treasurer in the leadership of the Youth Group. After a while, it came to our notice that this young person was repeatedly embezzling the funds of the Youth Group. We made several attempts to rectify this situation quietly, but to no avail. This young man would not heed our council and demonstrated no remorse or repentance for what he had done. Our appeals intensified, we fasted and prayed, but he was evidently entrenched in his deception. One morning in the midst of the conflict I felt that God had spoken to me. I was standing at our kitchen sink, drying some dishes, when a verse was powerfully emblazoned on my mind,

'It is time for judgement to begin with the house of God!'
(1 Peter 4:17)

At that moment I realised that as a leadership we were required to make a judgement on this issue, and pass an appropriate sentence. As a result of this, I spent several days examining the biblical basis for judgement and discipline. When I was clear as to what this entailed, I talked it through with the other leaders, and then initiated a course of action. We gathered the church and I taught the principles outlined by both Jesus and the Apostle Paul. At the end of my teaching, I explained the conflict we had been having with the young man in question, and that we now had to ask him to withdraw from the church until he was willing to both repent and demonstrate some restitution for what he had done.

It was at this point I learnt some very hard lessons. As long as our teaching is theoretical it will produce little reaction. However, when you actually do something to implement what is being taught, it can stir up all kinds of negative reaction in the congregation. My friend Maurice Smith used to say,

> 'Deal with the wolf in sheep's clothing and suddenly the "Wolf protection society" will come out of the woodwork.'

Now I know that church leaders can sometimes be very heavy handed and lacking in grace when it comes to disciplinary matters, but all too often the opposite has been true. A 'live and let live' humanistic philosophy has seeped into the life of the Church. We have become 'Peacekeepers' instead of 'Peacemakers'. I'm constantly reminding people that Jesus brought about reconciliation, *'... by making peace through his blood, shed on the cross'* (Colossians 1:20). Peace-making is often a bloody business!

After more than thirty years, I am convinced that the principles we embraced then, and the course of action we pursued, was a very necessary part of our development. To this day I struggle with churches that will not be open about misdemeanours, but prefer to sweep them under the carpet. All too often these are like festering sores, covered by a Band-Aid, that continue to rob the Church of God's blessing for generations to come. Proverbs 28:13 says,

> *'He who conceals his sins does not prosper, but whoever confesses and renounces them finds mercy.'*

This can be as true for a congregation as it can be for an individual. I can't begin to tell you the numerous examples of botched up attempts at discipline that I have encountered during my ministry.

Let me highlight the Scriptures that I feel are especially important here. In Matthew chapter 7 Jesus says,

> *'Do not judge, or you too will be judged. For in the same way as you judge others you will be judged, and with the measure you use, it will be measured to you.'*
>
> (Matthew 7:1–2)

This is one of those scriptures that people are fond of quoting out of context. Jesus is not saying 'Don't judge'. Later in the chapter He makes it clear that we must judge false prophets for example (Matthew 7:15–23). He is saying that we must be careful that we are not accusing others of faults while failing to deal with inconsistencies in our own lives. Once we do this, '*... then you will see clearly to remove the speck from your brother's eye'* (Matthew 7:5).

I was once given a booklet written by a high profile Christian leader in Australia that was a diatribe against homosexuality. This leader had presented his booklet to all the members of the Australian Parliament. Reading it, I felt distinctly uncomfortable. The book was almost pornographic in its descriptions of homosexual behaviour. Later, I learned that this leader was in fact a serial adulterer, who used his position to manipulate women. No wonder the Gay community often hates the Church for its hypocrisy!

In Matthew chapter 18 Jesus provides us with a clear course of action:

Step 1

> *'If your brother sins against you, go and show his fault, just between the two of you.'*   (Matthew 18:15)

In other words, don't invite your prayer partners to pray over this matter. That is thinly disguised gossip! Seek to deal with the matter personally and privately. This will give the person the opportunity to present their side of the story, which might be totally different from what you have understood. Your action will prevent it getting into the public arena and causing a lot of damage. When a tabloid newspaper prints an exposé of public figures, it may be inaccurate, but nevertheless a nasty stigma remains.

If a sin has been committed – and I mean a 'sin', not an infraction of personal or cultural preferences – even if it is not directly against you, but you become aware of it, you must take responsible action. James says,

> '... if one of you should wander from the truth and some-one should bring him back, remember this: Whoever turns a sinner from the error of his way will save him from death and cover a multitude of sins.'   (James 5:19–20)

Step 2

The aim of Step 1 is to entreat and win your brother or sister over. Obedience to this simple step alone would save an awful lot of problems. But failing that, Jesus says,

> 'If he will not listen, take one or two others along, so that every matter may be established by the testimony of two or three witnesses.'   (Matthew 18:16)

It is important at this point to mention Paul's instructions to the young Timothy,

> 'Do not entertain an accusation against an elder unless it is brought by two or three witnesses.'   (1 Timothy 5:19)

The high profile nature of leadership means that individuals can sometimes carry an unwarranted grudge against them, and this caution by Paul is presumably a safeguard against this. He does go on to say however, that,

> 'Those who sin are to be rebuked publicly, so that the others may take warning.'   (1 Timothy 5:20)

The public trust and responsibility of leadership carries with it a public accountability.

Once again, the aim of this meeting with other witnesses is to get the individual to listen, and hopefully respond to the admonition. Reconciliation should always be our prior concern, as long as there is evident repentance and a willingness to make restitution, and assuming that we haven't completely got the wrong end of the stick. I have sometimes thought that the gift of suspicion, a quality not mentioned in the New Testament, is often prevalent in the Church today.

Step 3

When the first two attempts have failed to reach a satisfactory conclusion, a more radical step is encouraged. Jesus says,

> *'... tell it to the church.'*   (Matthew 18:17)

Only twice in the Gospels does Jesus use the word 'church'. In Matthew 16:18 the Universal Church is obviously in focus. Jesus is not expecting the Church world-wide to be addressed with an individual's sins, though in these days of the Internet, this is more feasible, if not desirable. It is at the level of the local church that a person must be held accountable. Even at this more drastic stage, the hope is that the errant individual will humble themselves and listen to the body of believers. Failure to do so means that we must then,

> *'...treat him as you would a pagan or a tax collector.'*
> (Matthew 18:17)

Christians are often unsure what this really means. I would suggest that we must preach the Gospel to tax collectors and pagans. Failure on the part of an individual to heed the entreaty of the church suggests a fundamental lack of grace in their lives. It is in this context that Jesus goes on to speak of 'binding and loosing' and the prayer of agreement (Matthew 18:18–20).

Step 4

It is a rare thing to find a local church that will be as 'upfront' as Jesus encouraged us to be in Step 3. Sadly, Step 4 is often entirely overlooked. It has to do with the church functioning in spiritual authority. To 'bind' is literally to 'forbid', to loose means to 'permit'. When a church has exercised a necessary spiritual discipline, all too often, the individual is allowed to roam free without any further restraint. I am convinced that a corporate prayer of agreement, 'binding' the activities of the miscreant, could bring about an important spiritual embargo, rather than the freedom to continue perpetrating the offences.

When I first taught these principles, a member of the congregation told me of an experience that he had while serving with the British Army. He was stationed in Cyprus, and on the camp they had an active Christian fellowship. During his time there, a soldier who was a practising homosexual joined himself to the group, and caused a lot of difficulty and embarrassment by trying to seduce various members of the fellowship. Unsure as to the best way to handle this, the leadership team wrote to the governing body of the Christian network in London. The officer who responded pointed them to the Apostle Paul's instructions in 1 Corinthians chapter 5. He said that if there was no genuine repentance, they should,

> '. . . put out of your fellowship the man who did this.'
>
> (1 Corinthians 5:2)

The leadership team followed this wise counsel with dramatic results. When the homosexual man was alienated from Christian fellowship, he found himself friendless and ostracised by the rest of the soldiers. In misery, he committed a crime and ended up in 'the glass house' – the army prison. Having sunk so low, he cried out for God's mercy and forgiveness, and found deliverance in prison. Today, this man is happily married with four children and is serving the Lord in full-time Christian ministry!

Paul's teaching here in 1 Corinthians chapter 5 is particularly helpful. He is having to deal from a distance with a very alarming set of circumstances. A case of incest is going un-judged and unrestrained. Paul has no hesitation in telling the church exactly what they must do. He says,

> *'Even though I am not physically present, I am with you in spirit. And I have already passed judgement on the one who did this, just as if I were present.'*
>
> (1 Corinthians 5:3)

It is quite evident from this that Paul was not afraid to 'take the bull by the horns'!

> *'When you are assembled in the name of our Lord Jesus and I am with you in spirit, and the power of our Lord Jesus is present, hand this man over to Satan, so that the sinful nature may be destroyed and his spirit saved on the day of the Lord.'* (1 Corinthians 5:4–5)

Even such drastic measures as this are with a view to the ultimate salvation of the individual! In other words, when the person is delivered to Satan, removed from the protective care of the gathered church, there is the possibility of redemption from the extreme circumstances. Psalm 116 contains a desperate cry for mercy and an assurance of God's forgiveness:

> *'...when I was in great need, he saved me ... For you, O Lord, have delivered my soul from death, my ears from tears, my feet from stumbling...'* (Psalm 116:6, 8)

Paul makes it clear in this chapter that we must distance ourselves from Christians who are evidently living with double standards. He says specifically,

> *'...that you must not associate with anyone who calls himself a brother but is sexually immoral, or greedy, an idolater or a slanderer, a drunkard or a swindler. With such a man do not even eat.'*   (1 Corinthians 5:11)

If we fail to exercise spiritual discipline and judgement within our leadership team and the church, we will inherit three residual problems. The first has to do with **permeation**.

Paul says,

> *'Don't you know that a little yeast works through the whole batch of dough?'*   (1 Corinthians 5:6)

If we fail to deal clearly and cleanly with evident sin, it will insidiously work its way like a cancer through the body of the church. The whole principle of sowing and reaping applies here.

The second problem has to do with **redemption**. If we don't become pro-active in dealing with apparent sin, we are not making room for the redemptive process. In other words, we are not allowing that individual the opportunity to get right with God. It's interesting that Hebrews describes discipline as a mark of sonship. To not be disciplined is a mark of illegitimacy (Hebrews 12:5–11).

The third problem is perhaps the most compelling of all. It concerns the unpopular concept of **retribution**. If the Church fails in its God-given mandate of discipline and judgement, we are storing up retribution for the final day. People won't get away with their sins, even though they may think that they have! I would hate someone to turn to me and say, 'Why didn't you tell me?'

The New Testament repeatedly warns us about future judgement. Challenging His own disciples with the true cost of their discipleship, Jesus says that when He comes in His Father's glory, *'...he will reward each person according to what he has done'* (Matthew 16:27).

Describing this moment, Paul says,

'We must all appear before the judgement seat of Christ, that each one may receive what is due to him, for the things done while in the body, whether good or bad.'
(2 Corinthians 5:10)

Just think of the many tragic situations we might be able to prevent if we took the teaching of Scripture on this important issue to heart.

Over the years, I have had to be involved in so many situations that required a clear judgement and course of action. Some were thankfully successful and redemptive. Others remain amongst the most painful experiences in more than thirty-five years of Christian ministry. There are five crucial elements that I look for in this whole process. I have designated them the five 'Rs'.

- Repentance
- Remorse
- Restitution
- Recovery
- Reinstatement

Repentance

Christchurch Prison in New Zealand has a special unit for sex-offenders. Some years ago, the Christian director of this unit was addressing a ministers meeting in Auckland. He said that when an offender becomes emotional in his office and sheds apparent tears of remorse, he had learned not to place too much reliance on this performance. In his view, the prisoner had just 'wet his pants' because he had been found out. In the main, sexual offenders don't volunteer the information, they are found out! We must always take the time to find evidence of true repentance. Often we are in too much of a hurry.

Remorse

Paul says,

> *'Godly sorrow brings repentance that leads to salvation and leaves no regret, but worldly sorrow brings death.'*
>
> (2 Corinthians 7:10)

A mark of genuine remorse, is that there is no self-justification. When someone uses language that says, 'You failed to do this' or 'Someone should have done that', you know that the person you are trying to help has not come to true repentance. Get them to meditate in Psalm 51, David's penitent prayer. They won't find any cause for self-justification there. All sin is first and foremost against God, and we must say with David,

> *'...you are proved right when you speak and justified when you judge.'*
>
> (Psalm 51:4)

Restitution

This is an important part of the Gospel that is sadly often omitted from much evangelistic preaching today. In the words of John the Baptist we are to,

> *'Produce fruit in keeping with repentance.'* (Luke 3:8)

John goes on to tell the crowds that followed him that they must put right what is wrong. One of our first new converts in New Zealand owned a substantial garage business. When he became a Christian, he confessed a number of fraudulent insurance claims where he had deliberately crashed cars. His restitution involved a frank confession and a reimbursement of a considerable amount of money.

Recovery

The process of recovery will require submission to discipline without divisiveness. When someone in this process begins to 'play off' one person against another, or wriggles out of any accountable relationship, you know that something is foundationally wrong. At times like this, well meaning Christians can move towards such a person with sympathy but not discernment. If they are not clear themselves about the importance of the disciplinary process, they can negate it's effectiveness. Paul's prayer for the Philippian Christians is very apt at this point,

> '... *that your love may abound more and more in knowledge and depth of insight, so that you may be able to discern what is best and may be pure and blameless until the day of Christ...*' (Philippians 1:9–10)

Reinstatement

Some years ago, I was having supper with John Wimber, former leader of the Vineyard Churches, and his wife Carole, at a friend's house. During our discussion, John expressed doubt that a leader who had experienced serious moral failure could be re-instated to their former role. Since then, I have seen that John did actually do this with a key person in his movement, so perhaps he later modified what was a fairly strong opinion that he shared with me on that occasion. However, I fully understood his reluctance in the light of the betrayal of trust that such a failure represented. I wouldn't go as far as to say that it can't happen. In the Old Testament, David paid a heavy price for his sin and sowed destructive seeds into the future of the monarchy in Israel. But his penitence was very evident, and his love for God demonstrated the reality of Jesus words to the hardened Pharisee,

> '... *he who has been forgiven little, loves little.*'
> (Luke 7:47)

What we must not do, as I have already said, is be in a hurry. Let repentance do its thorough work.

In all that I have shared in this chapter, it is important to emphasise the need for clear communication. If serious sin is not clearly and cleanly dealt with, including appropriate levels of communication to those concerned, rumour and gossip can actually do more damage than the original offence. The worst thing that can happen though, is that we do nothing. If we fail to face up to our responsibilities in this area, we will never build a successful team.

Chapter 11

Winning

Someone once said to me: 'There's no such thing as a good loser!'

While the good loser idea may be important in terms of our attitude and sportsmanship, when it comes to winning games, a team needs to maintain a strong competitive edge to succeed. It is all about winning. Being part of a team that constantly loses can be very demoralising. Before you dismiss this as an unspiritual attitude because Christians have always felt that they were called to be the doormats of the world, think of the Apostle Paul's motivation,

> '. . . one thing I do: Forgetting what is behind and straining towards what is ahead, I press on towards the goal to win the prize for which God has called me heavenwards in Christ Jesus.'
> (Philippians 3:13–14)

I used to coach soccer, and when we first moved to live in New Zealand, I soon discovered that I was a commodity in short supply down under. Most of the children there had been raised on the wrong shape ball! Now, with parental concerns about the serious, injury-prone game of Rugby, the scene is shifting. More and more children are taking up soccer. This is also true in the United States where American Football also fuels parental fears!

In England I had coached Bristol Boys, a city-wide Junior team. In New Zealand the standard was nowhere near as high, so I quickly achieved winning teams. My two sons, Richard and Simon, both played for teams I coached. I remember one game when I was on the touch-line watching Richard play. He was in a half-back position and had not had the thrill of scoring a goal all season. I know you shouldn't do this, but I did it anyway! I prayed that he would score a goal. I just said, 'Lord, I would love Richard to score!' At that moment he launched a mighty kick from around the half-way line, and it bounced over the goal-keeper's head into the net! You may feel that this is a little unfair, and I don't recall using this tactic on any other occasion, but I was so pleased for Richard, and sheepishly thanked the Lord as the teams regrouped. There's something about scoring that's so important. Being a winner, or part of a winning team, does wonders for you!

My friend Wayne Drain, the prophetic singer and musician from Arkansas, USA, once wrote a memorable song on this theme, entitled 'We're gonna win'. To succeed, you must establish a **winning attitude** in your team.

Some years ago I had the privilege of attending a two day seminar in Auckland entitled 'The Psychology of Winning'. The motivator was Dr Dennis Waitley, a man who had helped prepare the American Astronauts for the Moon Landing. Listening to him I could understand why American athletics teams did so well at the Olympic Games. He had helped condition many of the United States athletes, long before many other countries had understood the importance of mental attitude alongside physical fitness and skill.

When it came to the Gospel, Paul was convinced that he had the best product in the market place. He said,

> *'I am not ashamed of the gospel, because it is the power of God for the salvation of everyone who believes ... '*
>
> (Romans 1:16)

If we're ashamed of our product, it's unlikely that we'll win anything or anyone. You must be convinced that you've got the goods and are able to deliver! When our team gets on the field of play, we need to know that we're unstoppable. Two years ago Linda and I were walking down 5th Avenue in New York when we came across the famous Presbyterian Church where Dr Norman Vincent Peale was the minister for fifty two years. Dr Peale's books, epitomised by *The Power of Positive Thinking*, influenced a world audience. A plaque outside the church said,

> 'He taught that positive thinking when applied to the power of the Christian message, could not only overcome all difficulties, but also bring about triumphant lives.'

Developing a positive attitude in harmony with the great truths of the Gospel is an important mind-set for a winning team.

Most of what I have written in this book uses the metaphor of team sports, not simply individual competition. In a team, everyone needs to know their position and primary function. A goalkeeper in soccer or a full-back in Rugby, are not usually spearheading the attack, but they have to be reliable in defence. A creative, attacking team, with the ability to score, needs to be supported by reliable defence, otherwise the team will quickly lose its morale. In soccer, not everyone's a striker – good ones are often in short supply. We've all seen the team that can do everything except get the ball in the net. But strikers can't score unless the team behind them has created the winning plays that put them in front of the goal.

In the early chapters of Acts, Peter was God's striker, but he needed the team and the supporters. We must recognise these gifts and make room for them. In 1 Corinthians, Paul gives a lot of consideration to different gifts and team function. He likens the Church to a body made up of very different parts, but with complimentary functions and a common purpose. He says that,

> *'God has arranged the parts in the body, every one of them,*
> *just as he wanted them to be. If they were all one part,*
> *where would the body be?'*   (1 Corinthians 12:18)

A player who hogs the ball all the time can be a real
nuisance. We must make room for each other and encourage one another towards the goal.

These days, top soccer managers devote a lot of time and
resources to study the opposition before they face an
important game. With satellite and video communications,
and easily accessible air travel, coaches and teams can study
their opponents at first hand long before they come face to
face with them on the pitch. They learn their tactics,
identify their strengths and weaknesses, determine to mark
exceptional players and develop strategies to penetrate their
defence.

When a team steps onto the field they know that their
objective is to score goals, and that they are facing an
opposition equally determined to stop them doing this.
This opposition wants to prevent their success, and at the
same time penetrate their defence in order to win the game.
Young leaders quickly discover what the Apostle Peter
describes so graphically in his first letter:

> *'Be self-controlled and alert. Your enemy the devil prowls*
> *around like a roaring lion looking for someone to devour.'*
>   (1 Peter 5:8)

Watching the last soccer World Cup Series, it became
more apparent just how important Peter's exhortation to
'be self-controlled' is. Highly paid professionals with cult
status and media attention can destroy their team's chances
by rash moments when they lose their self-control. Teams
now deliberately exploit such weaknesses in the hope of
gaining a penalty or a sending off. Managers often rely on
older, more experienced players to calm things down when
it looks like things are getting out of control.

This all becomes compounded when we realise that in

our teams we are not struggling against flesh and blood, mere human opposition, but a whole range of demonic adversaries that Paul calls, '... *the powers of this dark world ... the spiritual forces of evil in the heavenly realms'* (Ephesians 6:12).

This is why prayer cover is so important when we take on the opposition. The Apostle Paul was very conscious of the forces ranged against him as he sought to push out the frontiers of the Gospel, saying '... *we are not unaware of his* [Satan's] *schemes'* (2 Corinthians 2:11). The authorised Version of the Bible translates this, 'We are not ignorant of his devices.' When I started out in Christian ministry, I was almost totally ignorant of the devil's tactics, but I quickly discovered that we were up against some serious opposition.

What can be particularly difficult for a team is when there is a player who persistently lets the side down. Soccer manager Alex Ferguson, who I have referred to several times in this book, describes the painful decisions required to dismiss a very gifted player whose life is out of control in some area. Holding on to such a player can jeopardise the success of the whole team.

A recent experience of this involved a particularly gifted young guy who just couldn't keep his hands off the girls. The complaints were many and the incidents escalated. There were always plausible explanations, but no real repentance, and it was inevitable that we parted company. Not only does the Church have more than its fair share of peace-keepers – people afraid of confrontation – but at times God's people seem to be incredibly naïve. People in the world quickly pick up on these inconsistencies, while we live with glaring problems that no one seems willing to address.

All of us will make mistakes and have issues in our lives that need adjusting. The young people on our teams will face all the temptations that we have had to face as well. You quickly discover who is teachable and who isn't; who covers their sins as opposed to those who confess and forsake them. A player who repeatedly lets the team down is a serious threat to the morale and well-being of everybody. Like the heavenly gardener in John chapter 15, be prepared to prune fruitful branches, but also be ready for the more drastic measure of cutting off the ones that are unproductive (John 15:2).

Having encouraged a winning attitude at the outset of this chapter, I'm now going to flip the coin and present a more biblical view of success. God's ways are not our ways, and His strategy for defeating the opposition and scoring the winning goal took everyone by surprise!

I recently saw an old movie in which Robert Redford played a professional poker player. He made a very interesting observation during the film when he said that a professional card player will sometimes deliberately lose a winning hand to lull the opposition into a false sense of security, and later gain a much greater advantage! When I reminded Linda of this quote, she recalled having read somewhere that if the devil had known what Jesus would accomplish at the cross, he would have cut down every tree in Israel!

When Jesus set His face steadfastly to go to Jerusalem, telling His disciples beforehand that He would be betrayed, arrested and crucified, He met with a solid wall of opposition from even His most trusted friends. Peter, in one breath confesses Jesus to be the Christ, and soon after becomes the mouthpiece of Satan opposing the purposes of God (Matthew 16:13–28).

To the natural mind, Jesus' journey to the cross seemed a declaration of defeat, hardly best-selling material for the latest success manual. When the darkness finally fell and the disciples had all fled, it seemed that all of their hopes and aspirations had been destroyed. The poignant story recorded by Luke of the two disciples walking to Emmaus, leaving the scene of the great let-down behind in Jerusalem, says it all:

> '...*they crucified him; but we had hoped that he was the one who was going to redeem Israel.*' (Luke 24:20–21)

The thing I love in this story is that somehow these two men were kept from recognising Jesus. The faux pas of all time must have been when they said to him,

> *'Are you only a visitor to Jerusalem and do not know the things that have happened there in these days?'*
> (Luke 24:17)

Was it with tongue in cheek and a wry smile that Jesus asked them to tell Him exactly what had happened?

Philippians chapter 3 is one of the pinnacles of the New Testament. Here Paul talks about his life ambition in serving Christ, counting everything else as worthless in the light of his primary goal. As far as the Jews were concerned, he was one of the privileged few, born with a silver spoon in his mouth, and yet he says,

> *'... whatever was to my profit I now consider loss for the sake of Christ. What is more, I consider everything a loss compared to the surpassing greatness of knowing Christ Jesus my Lord, for whose sake I have lost all things. I consider them rubbish, that I may gain Christ...'*
> (Philippians 3:7–8)

Was Paul a loser then? Yes he was. Like the poker player, he surrendered a winning hand for a much greater prize! He said that he now only wanted one thing:

> *'... to know Christ and the power of his resurrection and the fellowship of sharing in his sufferings, becoming like him in his death, and so somehow, to attain to the resurrection from the dead.'*   (Philippians 3:10–11)

Later, as Paul encourages the Christians at Philippi to follow his example he begins to weep as he thinks of many who, *'... live as enemies of the cross of Christ'* (Philippians 3:18).

These are professing Christians, who own the name of Jesus, but refuse to take up His cross and follow Him.

The beginning of the New Millennium for us was tinged with sadness. One of our closest friends, Rachel Garratt-Pink, daughter of David and Dale Garratt, the 'Scripture in Song' pioneers, was battling a resurgence of a particularly virulent cancer. Only thirty-three years old, and with two young children – Ihaka, four years old, and Millie, just eighteen months – she and her devoted husband, Ramon, a medical doctor, bravely faced a very uncertain future. It was heartbreaking to watch Rachel deteriorate, especially for her family and friends, constantly praying for an elusive miracle. When she died on the 9th July 2000, it was in extraordinary circumstances.

Just two-and-a-half weeks prior to this, I had the privilege of conducting a simple ceremony in their home for the renewal of their wedding vows. Some seventy family members and friends packed into their lounge and kitchen to share in this emotionally charged event. Rachel and Ramon wanted to declare again their faithfulness to God and each other. It was difficult to know how to respond to this, as a young wife and devoted mother was evidently dying.

The next morning, Rachel and Ramon, with their son, Ihaka, and sister-in-law Vicki, flew out of Auckland to Los Angeles. Rachel wanted to take Ihaka to Disneyland and share with him some of the experiences that had delighted her as a child. They were also planning a consultation at a special cancer clinic in Mexico. Vicki later shared with us how Rachel went through a long list of all she planned to do with her on the overnight flight to America.

Having reached this point, most people in Rachel's circumstances would have given up, such was the rapid spread of the disease. Half way through their time in California, Rachel's parents, David and Dale, and her sister Melinda and daughter Millie, flew from Auckland to join the family in this unusual celebration of life. The testimony of them all was that, in spite of increasing disability and sleepless nights, Rachel sailed on with a determination to make the most of everything. When they finally boarded the plane to return home, Vicki realised that Rachel had done everything on her list.

During the many times of special prayer in the preceding months, Rachel's father David had often referred to the story of Esther in the Old Testament. Since her childhood, David had felt that there was an Esther-like quality about her life and character. Some weeks prior to this, the Lord had shown David, that like Queen Esther, the King had extended his Royal Sceptre to her, but that for Rachel this would mean being welcomed into His eternal presence. It was a devastating revelation. After sharing this with Ramon, David asked Rachel about 'making her petition to the King' one morning over breakfast in a Californian Deli. Rachel said that she had been planning to do this for some time and was waiting for the right moment. A few days later as they stood in the departure line at Los Angeles Airport, Rachel said to her dad, 'Maybe on the flight, I will go into the bathroom and present my petition to the King!'

Just over mid-way through the journey, Rachel asked for some oxygen as she was having difficulty breathing. She then asked Ramon to escort her to the bathroom and he said, 'I'll come in and help you.' Rachel said, 'No, you can't come in with me this time.'

Within a few seconds, in the privacy of that cubicle, she passed away. The King had extended His sceptre to her!

So, was Rachel a winner or a loser? In the eyes of so many in this world, she and especially her family, were definitely losers! To lose out in the prime of life, to be robbed of so much precious time with husband, children and family and friends, surely this is indisputable. And yet, as my daughter-in-law Katie said as she anchored Rachel's unique funeral service: 'She died at thirty-three, the same age as her beloved Jesus.'

To rightly assess the merits of winning or losing we must be clear as to what it is that we want to achieve. If business success and acquisition of wealth is the objective, then in the last few years, Bill Gates of Microsoft won the race hands down. If achievement of International fame and recognition was at stake, then the late Princess Diana led the field.

In the Sermon on the Mount, Jesus talks about the importance of rewards. Talking of religious hypocrites who fast, pray and perform acts of charity in public so that their righteousness can be seen by men, He makes the same comment three times:

> *'I tell you the truth, they have received their reward in full.'*
> (Matthew 6:2)

He goes on to demonstrate the futility of temporary, earthly objectives that are so short-lived and lacking in eternal quality. In other words, if that is the reward you want, make the most of it. It won't last very long! Jesus contrasts this with a worry-free life style, totally at odds with our frenetic culture. Rather, He says, we should,

> *'... seek first his Kingdom and his righteousness, and all these things will be given to you as well.'*   (Matthew 6:33)

As I have been finishing the closing chapters of this book, Sydney 2000 has come and gone, and in the words of International Olympic Committee President, Juan Antonio Samaranch, the Australians were assured they had, '... presented to the world the best Olympic Games ever!'

During those sixteen days, a small élite of the thousands of athletes who had converged on Sydney captured the coveted Gold medals. Years of endless training, discipline and sacrifice resulted in a moment of glory. They were winners, but apart from their appearance on the podium, the TV and press coverage, and a mention in the record books, it will soon all be forgotten!

Just prior to the opening of the Games, Shane Gould, Australian golden girl of the 1972 Olympics in Munich, spoke at a pre-Olympic forum at Sydney University. As a fifteen-year-old swimmer, she had won three Gold medals, but never competed at another Olympics, unnerved and overawed by a wave of publicity. Her words at the forum carried a solemn warning:

> 'Our culture suffers from championitis. The consumption of heroes is like psychological fast-food – un-nourishing, and a slow, deadly poison.'

She warned of the paradox of stardom, saying:

> 'A champion is not a champion without an audience, but that very audience can distract and destroy the champion, becoming the most seductive part of the champion's life. When a private identity becomes a public image it devalues inner-life and character. When saints become "stars" it devalues models of spiritual growth. When followers become "fans" it devalues discipleship. To be a champion one has to live in such a way that others can have a better life. By that yardstick, how many Gold medallists in Sydney will truly be able to call themselves "champions"?'
>
> (Quoted in the *New Zealand Herald*, Thursday 14th September, 2000)

At Rachel's funeral, everyone who spoke remarked on the simplicity and purity of her faith, the child-like trust she had in God, her single-minded determination to follow Jesus. Someone said she lived more in her thirty-three years than most people do in seventy! She powerfully impacted the lives of so many people. As we laid her to rest, an extraordinary fragrance lingered over the cemetery.

I mentioned Bill Gates and Princess Diana, who both achieved world-wide notoriety and success. Another high profile person from the last half century is the great evangelist, Dr Billy Graham, who has probably brought more people to faith in Christ than any other individual in history, including my wife, Linda. To know if you've won, is to know what you were aiming at in the first place!

> '*Do not store up for yourself treasures on earth, where moth and rust destroy, and where thieves break in and steal. Store up for yourselves treasures in heaven ... For where your treasure is, there your heart will be also.*'
>
> (Matthew 6:19–21)

There's only one way that we are going to win this game, and that is to adopt the tactics of our heavenly coach. We need a winning attitude, a determination to go for the prize, but Jesus said,

> '*... anyone who does not take his cross and follow me is not worthy of me. Whoever finds his life will lose it, and whoever loses his life for my sake will find it.*'
>
> (Matthew 10:38–39)

Dr A.W. Tozer once commented on this verse by saying that if you saw a man carrying a cross through a town or village in Israel, surrounded by Roman soldiers, you were sure of one thing: he was never coming back!

Chapter 12

A View from the Pitch

In November 1999, I had the privilege of re-visiting Sidcup to meet with the leaders and the church, and to interview some of the youth involved at The Worx. Things were really buzzing! I had just finished reading the Alex Ferguson's biography, *Managing My Life*, (Published by Hodder & Stoughton, 1999), and something evident in the strategy of Britain's most successful soccer manager was also coming through in Paul and Paula's leadership. The strength of Alex's teams have been undergirded by a vast talent-scouting operation and the development of their youth teams. Alex had learnt this from his hero, Jock Stein, the legendary manager of Scottish soccer team Celtic, and also the Scottish national team.

When Celtic were at the top of one of their most successful seasons in history, ten of the players came from a twelve mile radius of the stadium in Glasgow, and one, Bobby Lennox, came from thirty miles away in Ayrshire. As Alex Ferguson says, 'Jock won the European Cup with a Glasgow and district select.' He then took this concept on board, and despite the considerable resources of his team in later years to buy international players on the world stage, it was their youth stable of local lads that produced some of their best players!

One day, Paul Weston and I drove out into the Kent countryside and sat for several hours over a delightful meal in a country pub. He told me about 'Essence'. Paul and Paula had for some time called together a group of fifteen young people for a more intensive discipleship programme. This wasn't advertised. Most of the church didn't know about it. They would alternate leading sessions, working through the Pioneer leaders manual and other helpful material. Whenever they travelled out to speak at universities, churches, and special events, they would take as many of these young people with them as they could. Paul said they really needed a mini-bus for this, but couldn't afford one at present. The great thing with Paul and Paula is that they get on and do it, even when they lack the necessary equipment!

Paul gave me several definitions of the word 'essence': 'all that makes a thing what it is', 'an indispensable quality or element', 'an extract obtained by distillation', and 'an abstract entity, reality underlying phenomena'.

When they travel together, they make it clear that the young men and women going with them are not passengers. They are all expected to prepare themselves and get ready for involvement.

Anthony Henson, a leader of a church in Leicestershire, England, that had invited Paul to speak, said that when Paul mentioned he was bringing this team with him, he was really anxious that it wouldn't work. Afterwards, he declared that he was amazed by the impact of the team and gave them all an individual gift for coming.

The quality of these young people never ceases to surprise me. Two young men, Jon Rouse and Matt Carvosso, had both been banned from a local church youth group for being too disruptive! Over a period of three years, these young guys have emerged as some of our best leadership prospects. Paul encouraged me to ask Jon about an incident that took place at one of the recent events at The Worx.

One night, he told me, a crowd of young people were present from St. Peter's Anglican church in Hextable, Kent. The vicar had been encouraging them to come into events that we had organised for some time, and our Team had run several youth camps for them. This night, Paul said, 'We've got a crowd of folks in from Hextable, and I feel we should pray for them.'

With this, they got them all in the middle of the room, and symbolically wrapped them together with a huge roll of paper. Paul said, 'I want you to stir yourselves up to pray and prophesy over these people.'

As Jon Rouse stood there, a word dropped into his heart that gave him a few problems. The Lord said to him, 'There are two brothers here whose surname is Webb, and they need to be reconciled.'

Jon said to me, 'I bottled it for a while', then after ten minutes, during a pause, I said, 'Is there anyone here whose surname is Webb?'

No one moved! Jon felt highly embarrassed and the meeting moved on. Then the Lord directed Jon to look at a young man specifically. Eventually, he took courage and said, 'What is your name?'

The young man said, 'Paul!'

Jon said, 'Paul who?'

He replied, 'Paul Webb'

With this, Jon turned and pointed to another guy and said, 'And you're his brother and you need to be reconciled!'

With this, they broke down and came together, getting right with God and with each other.

Jon is only nineteen years old, but carrying a remarkable maturity of gift and ministry. He is currently doing a one-year training course with Pioneer called 'DNA', that gives both biblical and practical training with plenty of 'hands on' experience. With potential like this rising up in our midst, the future is very bright indeed.

Often, what younger people lack in maturity they make up for with passion. As Paul and I sat in the Chequers Inn that afternoon, we got into conversation with the chef and owner of the restaurant, Henrique da Silva. Although raised in Africa, Henrique comes from Portugal. As we talked, he highlighted for us the fact that the further south you move in Europe, the more passionate the people become about everything. Traditionally, Britain has been renowned for the 'stiff upper lip' attitude, but the more multicultural we become, the more we see this stereotype changing. This is particularly evident amongst the young people at The Worx. They are passionate about God!

For some weeks prior to my recent visit to Sidcup, the church had been engaging in twenty-four hour prayer. Every hour of the day was covered by someone, and at least two people met through each hour of the night. This was not just the youth, but the whole church and once again the passion for prayer was very evident.

Early one Sunday morning I made my way up to The Worx building to join in the prayer. Quite a number of people had maintained a vigil from midnight until four in the morning. By the time I arrived three young people were still there. In a corner of the building a special prayer tent had been erected. You climb through a porch into something resembling a Bedouin Arab's dwelling. There the similarity stops, because every available space – floor, walls and ceiling – is covered with unusual graffiti. There are scriptures, prophetic words, prayer requests, the names of people needing God's help, all in different colours and surrounded by drawings and symbols. The tent is partitioned and has cushions scattered around, including a foam mattress if anyone needs to sleep.

As you step into this tent, the thing that hits you is the atmosphere! For a long time you just want to sit, kneel or lie prostrate on the floor. This is a Holy Place where God has been meeting with His people. Often music will be playing from an appropriate CD. On the morning I was there, the powerful prayer of the Celtic Saint Brendan was echoing through the tent:

> Shall I abandon O King of mysteries the soft comforts of home?
> Shall I turn my back on my native land, and my face toward the sea?
> Shall I put myself wholly at the mercy of God.

Without silver, without a horse,
Without fame and honour?
Shall I throw myself wholly on the King of Kings,
    without sword and shield.
Without food and drink, without a bed to lie on?
Shall I say farewell to my beautiful land placing
    myself under Christ's yoke?
Shall I pour out my heart to Him, confessing my
    manifold sins and begging forgiveness, tears
    streaming down my cheeks?
Shall I leave the prints of my knees on the sandy
    beach, a record of my final prayer in my native land?
Shall I then suffer every kind of wound that the sea
    can inflict?
Shall I take my tiny coracle across the wide, sparkling
    ocean?
O King of the glorious heaven, shall I go of my own
    choice upon the sea?
O Christ will you help me on the wild waves?
                    (Recorded by Malc Garda and friends,
                        live at Revelation – Wave CD)

As I lay prostrate on the ground listening to this impassioned prayer, it struck me that it is this sense of reckless abandon to God and His Purpose that characterises all true works of faith. It was this spirit that I have encountered again and again in The Worx. The Celtic saints who have inspired us so much recently symbolised the Holy Spirit as the Wild Goose. As Michael Mitton says in his book *Restoring the Woven Cord*:

'Too many churches have wanted to domesticate the Holy Spirit keeping this Wild Goose caged and safe by imposing rigid and controlling worship styles (whether it be liturgical or free) trapping our meetings with bureaucracy and endless reports and feeding our people with tragically low expectations of what God can do in and through them. As we approach the third

Millennium AD, the Celtic church of the first Millennium wonderfully and joyfully challenges us to learn once again what it means to have a carefree spirit of adventure.'

On this Sunday morning three young people were present and we enjoyed a rich time in the presence of God over the next two hours. Jamie Garland is fourteen years old, Lucy King, seventeen, and Jess Harper, eighteen. It was interesting talking to all three of them, that Paul and Paula Weston had initially taken time to chat to them at various events they came to. Lucy first came to The Worx when she was fourteen to help paint some graffiti on the walls of the Arcade Room. She said, 'I didn't know it was a church, I thought it was a Youth project.'

One night, while she was playing pool, she heard about Firestarters – a special prayer event for youth in the area. She asked Paul about this and he said, 'If you come, I'll get you in for free.'

At that first Firestarters, Chris from Generation Church at Ewell, had a word of knowledge, 'Someone here wants to know God, but they feel that if they don't meet with God tonight, they'll never become a Christian.'

Lucy said she knew it was her, but struggled to respond. They all went out into Sidcup Place, the local park, to light some fireworks. Paula saw her standing alone so went over to talk with her. A few minutes later she prayed with her to receive Jesus. Lucy said it was like a new beginning.

Jess, on the other hand, came from a Christian family that moved up to Sidcup from Wales. She remembers sitting round a camp fire at a local scout camp when Paul asked her, 'What do you want most?'

Jess responded, 'I want to see revival.'

Like all teenagers, it hasn't been easy for her and she shared very honestly how she lost her way for a year, pursuing an unhelpful relationship. When this ended, she said it took several weeks to sort her life out, but now she feels back on track, still carrying a passion to see revival.

Jamie, the youngest of this trio, said he was always hanging around the back of the church and didn't want to get involved. Paul had recently joined the church and saw Jamie out on the fringe. He challenged him to really become a Christian and get fully involved. Jamie was twelve at the time, and in his words, 'started to really go for it!' For the last two years he has tried to be at every meeting and given it his best shot. At the Pioneer 'Event for Revival', Jamie got really fired up through the ministry of Ishmael and others. He said that in one of the main celebrations, he ended up holding the microphone and leading several thousand people in the prayers.

Two of these young people come from single parent families where 'Dad' is no longer around. Sad to say, two out of three is not an unusual average in Britain today. It's not easy for them to overcome the kind of pressures that they are facing. Getting them to pray for me was an awesome privilege. I was very humbled by the way that they cried out to God on my behalf. When I left The Worx later that morning I was walking on air. I see such hope for the future in the face of these young people.

The whole prayer emphasis that so many of these young people are being birthed into came out of a lot of pain for Paul and Paula. They were desperate for a baby, yet Paula was in the midst of a miscarriage. Paul, feeling very distressed, walked out of the hospital to sit on a bench in the park nearby. As he sat there, it was like he entered into a dialogue with the Holy Spirit. The Lord said, 'How much do you pray as a church?'

Paul said he felt a measure of self-satisfaction with this question as for many months there had been prayer at The Worx four nights a week. In the space of one week it looked good, but as he visualised a one-month planner opened before him, it didn't seem so much. Then he contemplated a one-year planner and the slots devoted to prayer now seemed comparatively small.

It was at that point that 'Intimacy' was birthed. Linda and I had returned from the Grapevine Conference, wanting to encourage some prayer and fasting. We found Paul all fired up with a radical plan to call the whole church together for prayer during the month of October. I have no doubt in my mind that this season of 'Intimacy' permanently transformed the life of our church as well as that of so many individual members. A special bonus has been that Paula has since been able to carry a baby full-term, and Charlie Weston is a little darling of a girl giving us all a lot of joy!

Elsewhere in this book, I have mentioned that Paul and Paula had to leave a church that found it difficult to contain them. Even Jon and Matt, who I've referred to in this chapter, made a similar sticky exit from this church, and would readily admit they were not without blame. But, one of the most encouraging developments in recent months has been the measure of healing that has been experienced in inter-church relationships. There has much mutual seeking of forgiveness and genuine acts of repentance – all of which are signs of an authentic work of the Holy Spirit.

Sometimes Paul uses very graphic, prophetic acts to highlight this healing process. One day, as he was praying in preparation for an evening meeting, he felt that God wanted to use an unusual sign. He brought a box of eggs to the meeting and declared, 'Some people need to break some shells tonight!'

As he was explaining this Paul held up an egg and crushed it in his hand. He said, 'There are twelve people here who have a problem with me and the vision that we are pursuing as a church.'

With that, the first person in line was a former member of the church, who had left long before New Generation was born. He confessed that he had come back that night after several years absence, just to tell Paul what he perceived to be the damage he was doing to the church! One by one the eggs were crushed that night! How often leaders have said to me, when confronting radical changes they need to make in the life of their church, 'I feel like I'm walking on egg shells!'

The time for procrastination has gone. If we are going to

restore passion and let fresh young leaders challenge our status quo, no matter how messy or fragile it may seem, we must act now! Doing it is doing it!

Back in the sixties, my friend Barney Coombs was leading a Baptist church in the south of England, when he had a very dramatic dream. During a time of fitful sleep, he saw himself walking down a narrow, sunken country lane with high hedges on either side. Barney, a former London policeman, is very tall, and he could see over one of these hedges into an adjoining field. As he watched, a ferocious beast raced towards the hedge holding a young spring lamb in its powerful jaws. As he watched, the beast sank its teeth into the neck of the lamb, and a large blood blister, the size of a balloon came up on its neck.

When Barney awoke, he was very perplexed by the dream. We have a mutual friend, Ronnie Wing, who over the years has exercised a remarkable gift of the interpretation of dreams, and so Barney decided at once to consult him. Ronnie likes to receive the dream written on a sheet of paper, without knowing the identity of the person who had it, so as to avoid being influenced or prejudiced in any way. He will then wait on God and often write the interpretation on the reverse side of the paper. In this instance, Ronnie's interpretation went as follows:

> 'The man walking down the lane is in a position of senior responsibility in the body of Christ. The beast and the lamb represent two factions within his sphere of responsibility. There is a lot of new life that could well be destroyed by the 'old guard' that the beast in this dream represents. The solution is for this man to get out of the lane into the field – he cannot hold back. He must rescue the new life from the jaws of the beast by taking a strong, positive lead.'

Ronnie went on to say that in fact, this dream was now in retrospect, and that the brother in question had already taken steps to get involved.

All of this was entirely accurate, including the fact that Barney had already for some months determined to release the church into the fullness of charismatic blessing. He became both passionate and resolute, unwilling to compromise the direction he considered necessary for the church to pursue. It is not surprising that this congregation has remained for so many years, such a powerful Apostolic resource church.

Barney and the generation that he and I represent, along with Paul and Paula and their emerging leaders have a similar characteristic. A willingness to take risks. John Wimber used to describe 'faith' as a four-letter word spelt R-I-S-K! A poem was once sent to me by Pete and Barbie Reynolds whose son, Simon, was tragically killed in an accident while on Christian service to the Black South African townships. They felt this poem summed up so much of Simon's attitude to life, and it certainly epitomises the quality of players I have seen on the field of play in Sidcup.

Risk

To laugh is to risk looking a fool
To weep is to risk appearing sentimental
To reach out for another is to risk involvement
To show feelings is to risk revealing your true self
To place your ideas and dreams before a crowd is to
  risk their loss
To love is to risk rejection
To live is to risk dying
To hope is to risk despair
To try is to risk failure
But risks must be taken because one of the greatest
  dangers in life is to risk nothing
Those who risk nothing, do nothing, achieve
  nothing, and become nothing
They may avoid suffering and sorrow
But they cannot learn, feel, change, grow, love or
  even live

Chained by their certainties, they are slaves
They have forfeited their freedom
Only a person who risks all that he cannot keep, to
  gain that which he can never lose ... is truly free.

Chapter 13

The Final Whistle

All games come to an end! We are already rapidly approaching the end of the first year of the new millennium. At its beginning I felt inspired to write a prophetic word for the year 2000 which I titled, 'The End is not the End!'

What do I mean? During the months of September to November, the Rugby Football World Cup, a four-year event, was hosted in Britain and France. During much of the last century, New Zealand with their national team, the All Blacks, have dominated much of International Rugby. Hopes were riding high for a repeat of their 1987 victory in the World Championship, but alas, it was not to be.

The semi-final against France at England's National stadium in Twickenham, upset all the bookmakers and commentators. One commentator in particular, New Zealand's Keith Quinn, probably wishes he could destroy the tape! It was just before half-time when the ball was thrown to the fearsome winger Jonah Lomu, already mentioned in this book in Chapter 7. He is huge, powerful, and very fast, so that what he may lack in defensive skill crumbles into insignificance when he runs toward the goal line with the ball. He seems to brush defenders off like flies, and on this occasion he brought the stadium, and the whole off New Zealand to their feet with a fantastic try! France had always been the underdogs, having lost all of their Five Nations matches, and for the All Blacks to establish a comfortable lead just before half time, the pundits could rightly imply that this was the beginning of the end. Keith Quinn obviously thought so! As he described Lomu's incredible try he said: 'End of story!'

After the half-time interval, the teams emerged for one of the most astonishing reversals in the history of International Rugby. France played like men inspired while the All Blacks fell apart! The final score of 43–31 to France left the nation of New Zealand numb as a pall of depression settled over the country. It was whispered that this defeat could overthrow the Government at the forthcoming General Election. Perhaps it did!

This chapter marks the end of my story, but of course, it's not the end! Biblical truth is eternal, and there is enough of that truth expressed in these pages to last the distance. But many things will be altered, and perhaps have been already, even as the ink is drying on the page!

On Wednesday, 24th November 1999, Paul Weston drove me to Gatwick Airport to catch my flight to the United States, something he has done on countless occasions. We always enjoy these journeys, and on this occasion there was sufficient time to have breakfast together after I had checked in. Over the meal Paul began to share with me a plan he had to help the older end of the church really find their groove. He, more than anybody, realised how easy it was for the long serving veterans to get lost in the pursuit of radical change with a primary youth focus. I was encouraged by the maturity of his perspective, even though he had at times expressed his frustration with some older people's lack of flexibility. Now he realised steps of adjustment needed to be taken.

There is a very important principle here. When I was a student of Physical Education at Loughborough College in England, we were taught the laws of motion. Basically it means that every time a body takes a step forward it is thrown out of balance. To compensate for this, there is an equal and opposite reaction in the other side of the body to bring it into balance before a further unsettling step is taken. In my early Christian experience I was part of the Inter-Varsity Fellowship, the umbrella organisation linking Christian Unions across Britain. I soon discovered that for a young Christian, their philosophy majored on the import- ance of being 'balanced'. That this often seemed to mean being very boring as well occurred to me early in my experience, and contradicted a lot of what I was soon to discover about the drama of an exciting faith walk. The person who makes no mistakes makes very little. Trying to steer a stationary vehicle is very difficult. A car on the move is easier to steer, but much more prone to accidents.

Looking back over nearly 40 years of my Christian walk I can see a number of times when I have been quite un- balanced. I'm sure that the radical steps we took at The Worx and with the re-birth of New Generation Church, were at times very unbalancing! Give us the time over again and we might well do some of it differently. We were not always as sensitive as we should have been. We took risks with young people, some of which have paid off and some of which haven't. Even the stories of individuals that I have recounted here, true at the time of writing, will no doubt change. Some will make it – some won't. That's life!

Last year we received a Christmas card from Dennis and Kay Fancett, an older couple who left our church in the midst of all this dramatic change. Some people leave the right way and some get it all wrong. For me, Dennis and Kay exemplified the way to make such a move. They had been with the church from its beginnings some seventeen years before and had served faithfully through that time, being renowned for their hospitality and generosity, and a genu- ine compassion. Try as they might, they couldn't find their place in what was happening, and felt the time had come for them to seek a new spiritual home. Dennis had been on the leadership team for most of the years that Linda and I had led the church. Instead of gossiping or undermining what we were doing, they would talk frankly to us about their problems. Clear communication at times like this is so important. Illegal communication is when we repeatedly share things with people who have no way of being part of the solution to our problems.

After many months of prayerful deliberation, Dennis and Kay felt they should leave. We were equally keen that they should not simply slide out of the church, but be sent. A verse of Psalm 121 has always carried special significance for me on such occasions,

> *'The Lord will watch over your coming and going both now and for evermore.'*　　　　　　　　　　　　(Psalm 121:8)

Another version describes this as 'going out and coming in' always particularly vulnerable moments for anyone. Whether it is leaving for work in the morning and returning in the evening, shifting home, changing jobs, or more dramatically, moving countries, we need to be specially careful how we go out and come in! At such times we are particularly in need of the blessing of God.

Dennis and Kay talked it all through with the leadership and a day was appointed when we would send them out. We encouraged them to share publicly what was on their heart with regard to their move, and the church responded with prayers of blessing and words of encouragement, as well as gifts of appreciation for all they had done. Personally, I was very sad to see them go, but understood the importance of the step they were taking. A mark of their commitment was that they continued to support the church financially for several months after they had left. Having been some of our most generous givers, this meant a lot to us. Also, I was able to meet the leaders of the church they subsequently joined, commending this couple to them with all sincerity. Their Christmas card to us said this: 'We went back to New Generation last week when Tom Gallagher was baptised – overjoyed to see so many new people there.'

Isn't it great that they could be 'overjoyed' with the success of the church. Here is a mark of godly transition: you genuinely want people to succeed. You are not secretly cursing them with your words and attitude.

I wish that I could say that we had handled all difficult times as well as this, but I can't. Many mistakes have been made along the way, and in some instances people have done us a lot of disservice. Not many though, I hasten to add!

But the end is not the end. We are still looking for that day, so graphically illustrated by one of the fishing incidents in the Gospels. Jesus, having borrowed Simon's boat to speak from when the crowd was so great on the shore of Galilee, repays the kindness with a miracle. When He tells Simon to put out into the deep water and let down the nets for a catch, the experienced fisherman is sceptical.

> *'Master, we've worked hard all night and haven't caught anything. But because you say so, I will let down the nets.'*
> (Luke 5:5)

Everyone knows the outcome of this expedition:

> *'... they caught such a large number of fish that their nets began to break.'*   (Luke 5:6)

It is the ensuing events of the great catch that are so encouraging, especially when you know how competitive fishermen can be!

> *'... they signalled to their partners in the other boat to come and help them, and they came and filled both boats so full that they began to sink.'*   (Luke 5:6–7)

If at The Worx we have achieved any success with the next generation, it is not with any sense of superiority, or indeed a desire for isolation from the rest of the Body of Christ. We're looking for a win/win situation. We want all the churches in our town to succeed so much, that we will all be overwhelmed with fish, and partnership will be inevitable! This is one of the reasons we are praying regularly for all the other churches in the town!

When I wrote the title of my prophetic word for the year 2000: 'The End is not the End', I had something else in mind that has special bearing on the youth we are trying to reach. I was thinking of Jesus' phrase in Matthew 24 as He prophesied the escalation of international traumas prior to his Second Coming. These things – wars, famines and earthquakes – are said to be,

> '... *the beginning of birth-pains.*'   (Matthew 24:8)

In other words, they are not 'the end' in the sense of termination, but as Greek scholar W.E. Vine points out, it means, '... the heading up of events to an appointed climax.'

Because God is eternal, He never ends, even as He had no beginning – a concept beyond the grasp of our finite minds. Paul says that,

> '... *the whole creation has been groaning as in the pains of childbirth right up to the present time.*'   (Romans 8:22)

He promises that:

> '... *the creation itself will be liberated from its bondage to decay and brought into the glorious freedom of the children of God.*'   (Romans 8:21)

I can't get excited about the disintegration of everything, but I can thrill to the thought of an emancipated creation – God's New Age!

Working amongst youth has taught us one thing: so many of them have lost hope! Consider the alarming escalation of teenage suicides in recent years. New Zealand, one of the most desirable and supportive places to live, still has one of the highest rates of teenage suicide in the world. Why is this? So many teenagers have lost all sense of hope.

I think there are three things we must provide for our youth if they are going to enjoy a satisfying future. These are not the only needs they have, but represent qualities in life that we must promote if the Church is going to have an effective ministry to future generations.

The first is **hope**, which will not be encouraged if we propagate a 'doom watch' approach to Bible Prophecy and the future. The second is **belonging**! An American prophet, Dale Gentry, once said in a meeting I attended in Westminster, that a primary principality over the City of London was that of loneliness. Amazing that in a city of twelve million people, so many feel isolated and alone. Young people need to belong. Elsewhere in this book I have talked about the importance of people: 'belonging before they believe'! Our churches must become welcoming places, intent on serving the needs of others, not satisfying ourselves.

Thirdly, this emerging generation needs **purpose**, a reason for being. We soon discovered that simply providing entertainment is not a key to a successful youth ministry. They need to be captivated by Jesus and His radical, pioneer plan for a new humanity. That dying we live; that losing our lives we save them; that being a servant is the way to rule. In terms of His earthly life, it was all over for Jesus by the time He was thirty-three. As far as His public ministry was concerned, it was a short, sharp, spurt of just three-and-a-half years. But He turned the world upside down in that time, or more correctly, right side up. As Isaiah the prophet declared,

> *'Of the increase of his government and peace there will be no end.'* (Isaiah 9:7)

What will be 'the end' of the story? Bob Mumford used to say, 'I've read the end of the book and we win!'

While that is true of the Bible and God's eternal purpose, what about us here and now? When you get to my age, you realise that your generation has had a fair crack of the whip and it's time to make room for others who will carry the baton triumphantly. Ian Oliver, who as Business Manager for Pioneer Events worked closely with me on the Event for Revival and the Event for History Makers, was discussing the subject matter of this book with me recently. He said, 'It's simple, isn't it? Just remove the super-glue from one end of the baton!' Ian is renowned for such comments, and this time I think he hit the mark. Some of us simply won't let go!

When the baton changes, our roles change. It's not that you are now redundant, but you have different responsibilities to fulfil. I love the picture of athletes who have run their leg of the relay, racing across the field to urge their team mate, running the final stage of the race, over the finishing line. The triumph belongs to them all!

It's so easy in life to be a good starter, but not a good finisher! As Jesus hung on the cross, He came to that awesome moment when He bowed His head and gave up His spirit with the cry,

> 'It is finished.'   (John 19:30)

Three times earlier in this gospel Jesus talks about the importance of finishing.

> 'My food ... is to do the will of him who sent me and to finish his work.'   (John 4:34)

> 'For the very work that the Father has given me to finish, and which I am doing, testifies that the Father has sent me.'   (John 5:36)

> 'I have brought you glory on earth by completing [finishing] the work you gave me to do.'   (John 17:4)

So when Jesus cried, 'It is finished', knowing that His life's ambition was to finish the work that God the Father had given Him to do, what exactly was finished? In terms of Jesus' sacrifice for sin, and His redemption of a fallen world, nothing can be added to, or subtracted from this. He was the 'once for all' sacrifice for sins (Hebrews 10:10). But in a real sense, a baton change was taking place at the cross! Two millenniums have passed since that definitive event that stands at the crux of history. Generation after generation of the Church has carried that baton seeking to secure the inheritance of the nations won by the redemptive triumph of Jesus at the cross. Talking about his own suffering to the church at Colosse Paul says,

> 'Now I rejoice in what was suffered for you, and I fill up in my flesh what is still lacking in regard to Christ's afflictions, for the sake of his body which is the church.'
> (Colossians 1:24)

In other words, the work of redemption is finished, but the outworking of that in terms of global evangelisation is not. Here's where we pick up the baton! Like His Lord before him, Paul could say,

> '...I consider my life worth nothing to me, if only I may finish the race and completing the task the Lord Jesus has given me – the task of testifying to the gospel of God's grace.'   (Acts 20:24).

In my previous book, *First Apostles, Last Apostles*, I devoted a chapter near the end to what I have called, 'New World Apostles'. Commenting on the great prophetic Psalm 110, I say this,

> 'Imagine this, the dawn of God's new age, ushered in by an army of youth arrayed in holy majesty. This holy army are like the dew, sparkling with all the freshness and fragrance of a new day. Across the earth, God is raising up such an army, and they will be inspired and led by young, "New World Apostles" who could easily be overlooked unless we have eyes to see and a heart to train and release them.'
> (pp. 127–128, Sovereign World, 1998)

The cry of my heart is that my generation will ensure that the baton is firmly placed in their hands with impeccable timing, and that we will do everything within our power to support them and cheer them on over the finishing line. Even if this is to be from a heavenly seat in the Stadium, as Hebrews 12:1 implies it might be, I want to be there, on my feet, shouting the loudest!

> *'Therefore, since we are surrounded by such a great cloud of witnesses, let us throw off everything that hinders and the sin that so easily entangles, and let us run with perseverance the race marked out for us. Let us fix our eyes on Jesus, the author and perfecter of our faith, who for the joy set before him endured the cross, scorning its shame, and sat down at the right hand of the throne of God.'*
>
> (Hebrews 12:1–2)

Debrief

As two football teams leave the field of play after a hard-fought match, imagine the different emotions in the two opposing changing rooms. These days, cameras and reporters will be on the spot, recording the scenes of elation or depression, the jubilation or the frustration. In the following days, the coaches and players will replay videos of the game, and it will be scrutinised thoroughly from every angle. Mistakes will be highlighted, lessons learned, glory basked in. The sports writers and commentators will provide their own particular spin. Heads may roll!

At a recent meeting of the London leaders of Pioneer, Laurence Singlehurst of Youth With A Mission, UK, presented a penetrating but very disturbing analysis of the effect of the post-modern philosophy on Christian young people today. He described it as 'enthusiastic dualism'. In the last few years discipleship training schools have found:

> '...that a young person can be prophesying at 5 o'clock, Friday afternoon, seem to be the most spiritual young person on the course, then go home at the weekend, sleep with their boyfriend/girlfriend, take drugs, get drunk, and come back on Monday, and once again seem to be the most spiritual person on the course. They can prophesy, pray and be outwardly, dynamically Christian.'
>
> (*Post-Modernity and the Christian*, Laurence Singlehurst)

In my own enquiries, I found a very similar pattern with other youth training organisations. Our problem is that an older generation of church leaders are often quite oblivious to what is happening, even with their own young people. Laurence goes on to say:

'In a post-modern mindset, whatever truth you decide to live by does not have to be consistent. Because truth has now become "pick 'n' mix", you can believe two things, even though they are in direct contradiction with one another. There is this capacity to live life in what I would call "episodes" or an "episodic lifestyle". This is influenced by the soaps and dramas ... which have no story, but just have one episode after another. People can, over time, live very differently from one episode to another.'

Before we sit down in the dressing room with our heads in our hands, ready to throw in the towel, we must remember that none of this has taken God by surprise! If Paul could declare against the backdrop of the Roman culture, *'I am not ashamed of the gospel, because it is the power of God for the salvation of everyone who believes ... '* (Romans 1:16), then we may be sure that our culture is no more unreachable than his was.

There is one word, not yet mentioned in these pages, that has significantly influenced all that has happened to us, and may well give us hope for the next generation

For some years in Pioneer, we have been seeking to flesh out the implications of a prophetic word that came to us as a movement during the 'Breaking the Mould' conference, also discussed earlier in these pages, in 1993. This had to do with **The Jacob Generation**.

During this conference we looked at the interaction between the different generations in our churches, likening them to the Old Testament trilogy of Abraham, Isaac and Jacob. God was repeatedly described as 'the God of Abraham, Isaac and Jacob' in the Old Testament. e.g. Exodus 3:6–15.

The whole of this book is about generational transfer. Within the Church at large we saw it as very unusual for the distinctive generations to be comfortably working together, pooling their complementary strengths, and compensating for each others weaknesses. Within our network, the 'Abrahams' were likened to those pioneers of faith who caught a glimpse of the Church restored to the purity and power of the New Testament model. The 'Isaacs' came into the inheritance of what a previous generation had fought to recover, but were often perplexed as to where it was going. But the 'Jacobs' represented an entirely new breed!

The fact that God also repeatedly describes Himself as 'the God of Jacob' as well as 'the God of Israel' should be a source of great encouragement to us all. Jacob meant 'supplanter' – a reference to the way in which he grasped his brother Esau's heel at birth and then sought in later life to steal both his birthright and blessing by his deceptive actions. That God should align Himself with such a dubious character, must give us all cause for hope when we consider our own failures, and the shortcomings of the new generation. That God would cause Jacob to become Israel, the father of His chosen nation, a prince and ruler is even more surprising. God's grace is constantly amazing.

Identity and emptiness was at the heart of his struggle. Jacob needed to find God for himself. It wasn't enough that God was the God of his ancestors. The deceptive lifestyle that he had led and the blessing and birthright that he had twisted from his brother Esau's grasp, may have given him material prosperity, but in no way prepared him for a showdown with death.

It is fitting that we conclude with an epic sporting event, an Old Testament Heavyweight Title Fight! In Genesis chapter 32 Jacob wrestles with a mysterious opponent who proves to be none other than the Angel of the Lord. Even when he dislocates Jacob's hip, enough to end most fights, Jacob refuses to let him go. In his pain he cries out,

'I will not let you go unless you bless me.'   (Genesis 32:26)

One thing I am confident of with this 'Jacob Generation', is that in spite of everything, they want the blessing of God. The Church may have failed them, religion may seem like an irrelevant smoke screen, but there is still a hunger for spiritual reality.

When it seems that the fight is all but over, a strange exchange takes place. The Angel asks Jacob a question:

> *'What is your name?'* (Genesis 32:27)

The significance of this question is not lost on Jacob. Many years before, when he had crept into his blind father's tent, disguised as his brother Esau, it was the one question that he dreaded. Isaac said to him, *'Are you really my son Esau?'* (Genesis 27:24). For Jacob to reply, *'I am'* meant that an awful lie was firmly embedded in his DNA.

Jacob stole the blessing that belonged to Esau. He felt that he couldn't be himself to receive his father's blessing, he had to be someone else. Now all these years later, confronted by the same question, Jacob cannot lie to God's Angel. A one-word answer is all that is required: 'Jacob!'

With this, a whole new vista of opportunity opens up. Can God take Jacob and make him Israel? Can He build his nation out of such questionable material? Yes, He can! God is looking for overcomers. He gives Jacob his new name, Israel,

> *'...because you have struggled with God and with men and have overcome.'* (Genesis 32:28)

Jacob called this place Peniel, which means the 'face of God', and he discovered that God's face was infinite grace! Of course, Jacob didn't actually see God's face. Some theologians contend that he saw Jesus (known as a 'theophany' – an appearance of Jesus in the Old Testament). Others say that he wrestled with an angel (based on the reference in Hosea 12:4). Even Moses was not allowed to see God's face (Exodus 33:20), and the Apostle John says that,

'No one has ever seen God, but God the One and Only
[Jesus], *who is at the Father's side, has made him known.'*
(John 1:18)

In my previous book, *First Apostles, Last Apostles*, speaking
of the young, New World Apostles I say,

' ... the present generation of youth from whom these
apostles emerge, is perhaps the most contaminated in
human history. The pollution that young people have
experienced everywhere through a relentless diet of
media manipulated sex, violence, drugs and broken
relationships has left them seriously scarred, even at an
early age. This army will need not just a baptism of the
Holy Spirit, but of fire as well, to refine and purify
them to reach our fallen world and restore it to the
image of God.' (p. 128, Sovereign World, 1998)

At least with this generation, there is not the hypocrisy
that so many previous generations of the Church have lived
with. Christian youth today have been completely demoralised and disillusioned by the moral failure of many senior
Christian leaders. World-wide, it's at epidemic proportions.
It seems that powerful, charismatic leaders, often author-
itarian and frequently unaccountable, have dropped the
ball very badly. Laurence Singlehurst calls it an 'episodic
lifestyle'. Veteran Christian Psychologist, M. Scott Peck, in
his book *In Search of Stones*, describes it as 'compartmental-
isation' – the ability to perform spiritual duties in one
compartment of our lives, and live in an entirely different
compartment when it comes to personal morality.

The supreme generational transfer highlighted by the
division of Testaments in the Bible brought us out of the
Old Covenant and into the New. This wasn't accomplished
by a set of new ideas, another set of rules, a new philosophy.
A bunch of young, rugged fishermen and tax collectors got
a glimpse of God. They saw the Word fleshed out before
their eyes. What Jewish tradition had failed to do for them,

and what the law could never produce in them, happened when *'The Word became flesh and made his dwelling among us'* (John 1:14).

In the movie *The Cider House Rules*, starring Michael Caine as a doctor running a dead-end orphanage in Maine, New England, there is a touching sequence at the end of each day. As he wishes the children 'Goodnight', and turns out the dormitory lights, he says to these tragic, rejected orphans, 'Goodnight you Princes of Maine, you Kings of New England.'

That's the Father's heart for this Jacob Generation – Kings and Princes! Not what they are, not what they have been, but what through grace they will become.

> *'Let us fix our eyes on Jesus, the author and perfecter of our faith ... '*   (Hebrews 12:2)

He started it and He's going to finish it. He's actually bringing many sons, just like Himself, to glory! (Hebrews 2:10).

Good night you Princes of Maine, you Kings of New England!

If you have enjoyed this book and would like to help us to send a copy of it and many other titles to needy pastors in the **Third World**, please write for further information or send your gift to:

**Sovereign World Trust
PO Box 777, Tonbridge
Kent TN11 0ZS
United Kingdom**

or to the **'Sovereign World'** distributor in your country.

Visit our website at **www.sovereign-world.org** for a full range of Sovereign World books.